THE ORIGINAL
NEW TESTAMENT
FOUND!

The Original New Testament Found!

Restored and Proven Identical
to the Original Autographs!

Found and Restored by
Rev. Glenn David Bauscher

Terry Lee Miller, Sr.

DISCLAIMER:
LET THE READER BE AWARE THAT THIS ASSOCIATION FIRMLY HOLDS THAT THE SCRIPTURES ARE ABUNDANTLY CLEAR THAT THERE IS NO SALVATION OUTSIDE OF THE NEW BIRTH INTO THE FAMILY OF GOD BY REPENTANCE AND FAITH IN GOD OUR SAVIOR THE LORD JESUS CHRIST. THIS ASSOCIATION ALSO HOLDS THAT THE SCRIPTURES TEACH EVENTUAL UNIVERSAL SALVATION FOR ALL MEN, "...AND EVERY KNEE SHALL BOW AND EVERY TONGUE SHALL CONFESS THAT JESUS CHRIST IS LORD TO THE GLORY OF GOD THE FATHER." WHILE IT IS NOT CLAIMED THAT THESE PAPERS ANSWER ALL QUESTIONS REGARDING POST MORTEM PUNISHMENT AND EVENTUAL UNIVERSAL SALVATION FOR ALL (AFTER THE WHITE THRONE JUDGMENT REV.21:4), THE FACT REMAINS THAT THEY CLEARLY SHOW THAT GOD IS THE ULTIMATE VICTOR OVER DEATH SIN HELL AND THE GRAVE. FURTHERMORE IT MUST BE REMEMBERED THAT THERE IS TERRIBLE SUFFERING IN PARTS OF HELL IN WHICH THE DESERVING UNSAVED DEAD CONSCIOUSLY SUFFER FOR THEIR SINS, AND AS WELL A REAL LITERAL HEAVEN INTO WHICH ONLY THEY THAT ARE TRULY BORN AGAIN CAN ENTER THEREIN. LASTLY, WE HOLD ABSOLUTELY NO ILL WILL TOWARDS THOSE WE TERM AS 'FUNDAMENTALIST DAMNATIONISTS,' BUT RATHER SEE THOSE WHO ARE DEDICATED TO THIS POSITION AS GOOD AND GODLY PEOPLE, BUT PEOPLE WHO ARE DECEIVED AND MISLED BY AUGUSTINIAN SO CALLED SCHOLARS. IT CAN TRULY BE SAID THAT THE STRONGEST AND MOST DEDICATED FUNDAMENTALIST DAMNATIONISTS CHURCHES USUALLY ARE THE STRONGEST AND BEST SOULWINNING CHURCHES, WITH THE MOST WONDERFUL DEDICATED PARISHONERS. THEY ARE USUALLY THE INDEPENDENT/BIBLE/BAPTIST/SOUTHERN BAPTIST PERSUASION. HOW MUCH MORE COULD THEY ACCOMPLISH FOR THE LORD, IF THEY WERE ONLY TO COME TO SEE THE TRUTH OF EVENTUAL UNIVERSAL RECONCILLIATION AND SALVATION FOR ALL MANKIND. ONE LAST WORD OF WARNING. THOSE WHO HAVE BEEN FIRMLY ENTRENCHED IN DAMNATIONISM AND READING THIS BOOK WILL FIND THEMSELVES GREIVED AND AGITATED, FROM HAVING THEIR UNDERSTANDING OF ENDLESS DAMNATION BEING CHALLANGED AND SCRIPTURALLY OVERTHROWN. WE INVITE THOSE WHO DISAGREE WITH THESE BIBLICAL FACTS TO SCRIPTURALLY REFUTE THEM, BUT THAT CANNOT BE DONE. WE ARE HONOR BOUND TO STAND ON TRUTH, NOT ON NEARLY 1500 YEARS OF AUGUSTINIAN CORRUPTION OF GOD'S WORD. OUR MOTTO PROUDLY STANDS, "TRUTH WILL STAND EXAMINATION

Copyright © 2023. All rights reserved. Rev. Terry Lee Miller Sr. D.MIN. Th.g
Christian Universal Redemption Baptist Association • C.u.r.b.a.

Published by Eternity Publications, 1252 Sessions Rd. Elgin, S.C. 29045. U.S.A.

Paperback ISBN 978-1-7350281-6-3

THIS DOCUMENT MAY NOT BE REPRODUCED IN ANY MANNER WITHOUT EXPRESS PERMISSION FROM TERRY LEE MILLER SR. OR HEIR.

This book was printed in the United States of America.

Introducing the Aramaic Original N.T. Holy Scripture — the Restored First Original Ancestor of Our Time Honored 1611 K.J.V. Translation and Other Decendents Based On the Textus Receptus

* The first original New Testament was given to the Apostles in Aramaic and not Greek in the first century, and immediately thereafter translated into the Greek and other languages. Aramaic was the native language of our Lord and his disciples as verified by Jewish historian Josephus.

* Rev. Bauscher has discovered divine codes and indisputable mathematic equations which as divine watermarks verify the authenticity of the divine text! No other religious text in the world has such divine codes. These codes etc., only come to light with super computer code analysis. Ruckmanism falls in ruins. Rev. Bauscher's Aramaic/English interlinear is a must for any Christian.

* To add one letter or word, or take away one letter or word to this Bauscher text and the codes disappear.

* This Aramaic text indisputably proves Jesus/Yeshua was literally God come in the flesh! Also it endorses the textus receptus/received text the linage and forerunner of the 1611 K.J.V. Translation.

* David Glenn Bauscher is a scholar/ master of the Hebrew, Aramaic, Greek languages. His web site includes many books. Go to https//aramaicnt.wordpress.net

Table of Contents

1. The Peshitta Original Bible Proves Jesus Is YHVH xi
2. The Original Apostolic Bible Restored the Inerrant Word of God 1
3. From Obscurity to Light the Aramaic Peshitta 9
4. To Destroy The Peshitta Bloody Persecution 17
5. Peter Ruckman False Apostle-False Prophet. 33
6. The Precious Invaluable Tetragrammaton. 43
7. Do Jehovah's Witnesses Believe In Jesus? 59
8. The Peshitta and The Divinity of Christ Jesus Yeshua. 71
9. The English Mastered In The Original Peshitta 79
10. The Divine 'Yah' of the N.T. 91
11. 'By The Mouth of Two or Three Witnesses…' 99
12. Thankfully Notice the Watchtower Unwitting Translation! . . .109
13. Jesus Accepts Divine Worship as YHVH/JHVH 115
14. Conclusion. 119

Acknowledgment

I am thrilled and extremely pleased to have the opportunity to write this booklet and offer it freely to the world. At the same time I must admit that I do not feel worthy to do this work. I am not a Bible scholar or theologian, but at best a student of the word of God for the past 60 or so years and am a strong personal soul winner. All of the praise, of course, needs to go to the Lord for using Glenn David Bauscher for the world shaking most important biblical discovery in the last 2000 years — 'the recreation/rediscovery/the restoration of the biblical manuscript which scientifically can now be proven to have only been originally written by the Apostles under divine inspiration. Yes that manuscript which he has restored is proven by codes and divine names etc., secretly and unknowingly missed by past non computer generations. Now however, by code finding programs under super computer analysis these codes etc., as divine watermarks, have come forth to prove its authenticity! This Bible now can be purchased from Rev. Bauscher on his web site https://aramaicnt.wordpress.net. Thankfully this gigantic breath taking discovery also spells the end of 'ruckmanism' and as well can easily silence atheist/agnostic/liberal skepticism as to whether or not the Bible is the true word of God or not. As well it puts all other supposed religious books/works etc., such as the book of Mormon, the Muslim Koran, the Christian Science Bible-Science and Health with Key to the Scriptures by Mary Baker Eddy etc, into the category of false theology. To those who doubt the truth of the above, just remember, "Truth will stand examination." — Rev. Terry Lee Miller Sr. D.Min, THG.

Jesus/Yeshua Plainly Identified as the Almighty Creator!

Nowhere in God's word does it state "Almighty God YHVH" bestowed upon a created being lesser than Himself, the infinite powers involved in the creation of everything visible or invisible. No! Quite the opposite. The Lord Jesus Christ the second member of the triune God head, fully therefore God with all of the attributes of Deity, was the one commissioned (not empowered) to design and create all of that which is/was created. As Almighty God the Son, being fully equal to YHVH Jehovah, He did just that!

Jeremiah 50:14-15-16

The Lord of hosts hath sworn by Himself... He hath made the earth by His power, He hath established the world by His wisdom, and hath stretched out the heaven by His understanding, when He uttereth His voice there is a multitude of waters in the heavens and He causeth the vapours to ascend from the ends of the earth: He maketh lightnings with rain and bringeth forth the wind out of His treasures." (KJV).

Nehemiah 9:6

Thou, even thou, art Lord alone; thou hast made the heaven of heavens, with all their host, the earth and all that are therein, the seas and all that is therein, and thou preservest them all; and the host of heaven worshippeth thee.

It must be stated that this manuscript would have been impossible without the works of Glenn David Bauscher, and helpfull notes of, Roy Reinhold and Ian Michaels. This manuscript is copyright August 2021 by Terry Miller Sr., 1252 Sessions Rd, Elgin, S.C. 29045, phone 803-438-4405. Please go to our web site 'universalchristiancurba.com' to download (for free) our literature (including this booklet). "The Death of Endless Damnation," "The Infamous Rapture Conflict Settled," "Abraham and the Trinity/Lot exonerated Gen. 18," "Calvinism and the Trojan Horse Within," and other valuable theological papers.

Introduction

THE PESHITTA ORIGINAL BIBLE PROVES JESUS IS YHVH

This author (myself) is convinced that Glenn David Bauscher will must go down as a most famous, God blessed servant of the Lord in all of church history! Brother Bauscher has uncovered/ and restored/ the original Bible/Word of God which was originally given to the Apostles under Divine inspiration. This discovery, the underlying codes, spiritual poetry, hidden texts, Divine names and other indisputable mathematical proof, can easily convince yea even an avowed atheist that God did indeed give us the Old and New Testament books for learning edification and winning lost souls to Christ! As well it proves to be the mirror image of the original Bible manuscripts as given by the Spirit of God though the apostles, and condemns all subsequent so called 'divine origin documents. As well it spells death to the false doctrines of Ruckmanism, doctrines which have so damaged the church. There can be no doubt that Ruckmanism is a satanic diversion away from and attack on the true one and only original Bible, the eastern Aramaic Peshitta Manuscripts. As well this Peshitta/Bible finally puts to rest just what is the master text by which to judge the slight differences in thousands of other Bible manuscripts from the first century until today! Only in this age of computers, could there have been such a discovery possible. Rev. Bauscher has used computer code programs to unravel the problems involved in closely examining the Aramaic Peshitta clearly revealing underlying watermarks if you will to reestablish the original text. So close and perfect this text is, to add or take away one letter or word makes the codes disappear! This discovery could only have been precipitated by Almighty God! Thank God for Rev. Bauscher. Following is critical information from his web site https//aramaicnt.wordpress.net (Also be sure to see his book on the underlying Bible codes found only in the Peshitta!)

Chapter One

The Original Apostolic Bible Restored the Inerrant Word of God

Rev. Bauscher's introductory information from his web site https://aramaicnt.wordpress.net

The original Aramaic New Testament (the Peshitta), so long asleep in the hands of a small middle-eastern group of churches, is now causing a movement of thousands worldwide who are returning to the roots of the New Testament. It's not just about returning to the spiritual beginnings of Christianity . . . to the land and language of Jesus and the disciples who were eye-witnesses of His ministry . . . but it's a revival and discovery of many passages of the New Testament which have hitherto been unintelligible or uncertain in meaning. It's the discovery of what was really said... Perhaps the greatest discovery being that which Jesus declared of Himself!

Only the Original Aramaic New Testament reveals that.

And only one Aramaic scholar can do that. His name is Glenn David Bauscher.

Since 1974, as a Greek scholar and researcher, Brother Bauscher has delved into New Testament textual criticism. It was his desire to find the purest transmission of the original New Testament. Here's what he found: (Following by Brother Bauscher).

"I'll never forget the day I came across the Aramaic Peshitta Bible. With a collection of manuscripts dating from the 1st century, it was something I couldn't ignore."

"I was convinced, after two years of intensive research, that the complete Peshitta New Testament was the original inspired text delivered to the apostles and evangelists."

While the apostle Paul was carrying the gospel message to the West — "first to the Jew, then to the Gentile" — Thomas was doing the same, except going in the opposite direction . . . to the East. The Church of the East became the largest Christian church of the middle ages, spreading the gospel message and building churches as far away as India and China, with 100 million members. The Muslim conquests and massacres of the 7th – 11th centuries, as well as the Mongol's destruction of Christians and churches, left very few members of that great church remaining. This is history unknown to most in the West, but eastern Christians have not forgotten.

So where does one find a word-for-word English Translation of the Original Aramaic New Testament?

Today . . . only two Aramaic scholars have presented a modern word-for-word English translation of the Aramaic New Testament. Only one is pursuing a complete Old Testament word-for-word translation as well . . . and that is Rev.Glenn David Bauscher. And it's not just an English translation. For those who want to see and compare the English to the Aramaic for truth and accuracy, Rev. Bauscher has prepared an interlinear edition as well.

The Original Aramaic New Testament (OANT) has:

Word-for-word verifiable accuracy in translation — which means you get the vocabulary, intent and meaning of the original New Testament author (and none of the translator's biases or interpolations).

A collection of notes — that emphatically demonstrates that the Greek New Testament was a translation from the original Aramaic New Testament. The complete set of notes comprises 200 pages . . . an entire book in and of itself!

A variety of formats to choose from — (soft and hardcover books, as well as electronic downloads) — which means you can select the medium, and the size, that suits you best.

Notice following, testimonials from students and scholars concerning this incredible Aramaic letter perfect translation of God's Word!

> "The world has long needed a complete Interlinear of the Peshitta Aramaic NT, and this fresh new translation proves to be an invaluable study tool for all Christians. After using this Interlinear for over 6 months, I can truthfully say that is has added more to my understanding of the NT than any other Bible version or tool. Take a look at the book review, and then get it!" — Roy Reinhold, Bible & Hebrew scholar/author

> "Thank you so much for the book, The Original Aramaic New Testament in Plain English. I am becoming more convinced through your work and efforts that the Original New Testament was in Aramaic and not in the Greek as many believe." — Randy, USA

> "I will promote the Peshitta in every talk or lecture I give and book I write from now on. . . . Timing is interesting given how close we are to the end times. . . . If I had the

money I would buy a dozen and pass them on to friends of mine." — Neville, Spain

"When I purchased your The Original Aramaic New Testament in Plain English, I started telling others about its incredible help and value to us who love the Word. . . . Here in the Philippines, we have a very large denomination, whose leaders strongly claim that Jesus is just a man, and not the Living God. I don't blame them now, because their source of original writing is Greek. Had it been Aramaic, they would know beyond any reasonable doubt that our Lord claimed DEITY indeed, and that He is indeed God the Son! — Kim, Philippines

"We all love your interlinear and most of us use it for our NT text. . . . We have told so many people about it and are constantly showing it to others and telling them how they need to get a copy! I found it amazing how much the harder passages to understand became so easy to understand!" — Samantha

"I have never been so excited over one single work till I found your publication!" — Danny

We want to give you as much history, facts, and resources as possible so that you can be informed and knowledgeable about the truth and origins of the Aramaic/Hebrew scriptures that we have inherited. That's why we've created this AramaicNT.com website and present you with affordable options to acquire your own copy of the Original Aramaic New Testament in print or digital formats. Get Yours Now! Go to https://aramaicnt.wordpress.net

Rev. Bauscher goes into further detail concerning his discovery of the original letter perfect Bible, provable by the divine coded Bible texts, which no human in any century could possibly have designed it into the divinely inspired text. He states as follows:

"It appears to me that God put these codes in the Aramaic New Testament to be discovered in the computer age, when many are skeptical and without faith in God or the Bible, but have faith in technology. There were no computers when the New Testament was written yet computer technology is required to find these codes I have found in the New Testament. Since no mere human, reading or studying the text could have found these codes without a computer, I affirm that no mere human in the first century or in any century before the computer age could have put them there, nor would he have reason to. It seems that the human difficulty of composing these codes would far exceed the difficulty of finding them. If the seven long codes (Rev. Bauscher has discovered- editor) are not proof enough, I have found millions of Divine Name codes in the N.T. via an experiment far beyond statistical chance occurrence numbers that pinpoint the Code maker's identity."

Rev. Bauscher further affirms the following:

1. The God and Christ of God of the New Testament exist and are exactly Who, and What that New Testament say they are.

2. The New Testament in which these scientific proofs exist is absolutely true in all its statements, i.e. infallible-historically, theologically, prophetically, scientifically, grammatically and textually-where it presents data concerning what pertains to the claimed statements and activities of God, Christ, and the Holy Spirit. Whatever statements of actions are attributed to humans, angels or demons are also accurately recorded and are true history, though, unlike Divine statements may not be necessarily true statements, since human and diabolical errors and lies are also accurately recorded.

3. The original New Testament was written in Aramaic and has been preserved to this day with 100% word accuracy in the 27 books of the Peshitta-Peshito form I have tested and in which I have found volumes of coded information.

4. Greek is not the original language in which any New Testament book was written.

5. The Greek New Testament is a translation of the original Aramaic text in all 27 books of the Western New Testament canon.

6. The number of letters in the original New Testament was and is 461,094, It is possible that the completed text as written approx. 1950 years ago had some few spelling differences in a few places or compound word division differences, but the total number of letters was the same.

7. God and His Son love you eternally and have provided for your eternal welfare and joy.

8. Nothing can separate you from that love. *(End Bauscher quote)*.

Preservation of Gods Word a Must
It must be stated here, that if God gave us a word for word, verbally inspired, letter perfect document called the Bible in the first century A.D. (which He did) and then allowed it (down through the centuries) to be permanently and irretrievably corrupted by any means at all, then such corruption would necessarily and potentially destroy any and or all truth contained therein, thus keeping all generations in darkness and on their way to Hell. The powers of Satan would have seen to that. God had to preserve His precious infallible word and as well make it available and provable to all generations. The Aramaic Peshitta underlying mathematics and coding does just that. Atheists,

agnostics and skeptics can now permanently be silenced! Thank you Brother Bauscher.

Another point is say (hypothetically) that there was no Mona Lisa original painting in existence. (The original is presently hanging in a museum in Paris). And further say 10 collectors of art had 10 copies of the same and all claimed theirs was the exact same as the original down to the smallest artistic detail, though they all differed in small important details. (These details vitally important to establish the value of their paintings.) Now pray tell who could possibly value one painting over the others since there would be no master print to judge them by? Yes it would be impossible! We have the same situation with the original autographs and our need to judge which extant N.T. manuscripts are closest to, or identical in information to the originals. Until now there was many times speculation by scholars on different N.T. manuscripts as to which ones were closest to the originals. Until now, there has been no available 'master,' which exactly mirrored the originals, to judge them by. Again, until now! Thank God for Brother Bauscher and his original provably so, Aramaic Peshitta complete perfect Bible!

Readers note: It needs to be added that over the thousands of years these 'differences' have existed, that not one 'difference' had any effect on any Bible truth or doctrine, God has seen to that.

Chapter Two

From Obscurity to Light the Aramaic Peshitta

So...Just What Is the Aramaic Syriac Peshitta?
No one can doubt that the original autographed New Testament scriptures were of infinite value to the early church. They were well aware of their superiority over all secular/historical/poetical etc. literature in the world! It is astounding and almost unbelievable that the average Christian (not to fail to mention theological schools), today are basically totally ignorant that the original New Testament manuscripts were written in Aramaic, (the common language of Jesus, his disciples and the Jews in the first century). No doubt the fact that they were so highly prized; they were immediately copied and translated into the Greek language within a few months after their arrival into this world in the first century A.D. That plainly was the will of the Lord when He said, "...the gospel to the Jews first and also to the Greeks." Later in this booklet is proof from Jewish Historian Josephus, that Aramaic was indeed the language of the first century Jews. The priests of that day considered Greek to be a profane secular language, and discouraged the young Jewish men from learning and speaking it. Of course they favored Hebrew in their worship and the Aramaic since both alphabets were identical. Added also, the Jews

adopted the Babylonian Aramaic language from being in Babylonian captivity for hundreds of years. After being translated into Greek, it was then translated into other languages, and as well was re-translated years later back into Aramaic from the Greek, (which explains why later extant Aramaic manuscripts slightly differed in very minute places from the Eastern Aramaic Syrian Peshitta.) Following is a quotation from one certain Catholic scholar who was absolutely honest concerning the origin of the Aramaic Peshitta: (Readers note: Though it is a Roman Catholic which reveals this, as Dr. Bob Jones Sr. said, "I do not care who turned the light on, I am happy it was turned on).

Patriarch Shimun XX1 Eshai

To this end, and in reference to the originality of the Peshitta, the words of Patriarch Shimun XXI Eshai are summarized as follows:

> "With reference to ... the originality of the Peshitta text, as the Patriarch and Head of the Holy Apostolic and Catholic Church of the East, we wish to state, that the Church of the East received the scriptures from the hands of the blessed Apostles themselves in the Aramaic original, the language spoken by our Lord Jesus Christ Himself, and that the Peshitta is the text of the Church of the East which has come down from the Biblical times without any change or revision."

In the first century CE, Josephus, the Jewish historian, testified that Aramaic was widely spoken and understood accurately by Parthians, Babylonians, the remotest Arabians, and those of his nation beyond Euphrates with Adiabeni. He says:

> "I have proposed to myself, for the sake of such as live under the government of the Romans, 'to translate those books into the Greek tongue, which I formerly composed

in the language of our country, and sent to the Upper Barbarians'. Joseph, the son of Matthias, by birth a Hebrew, a priest also, and one who at first fought against the Romans myself, and was forced to be present at what was done afterwards, [am the author of this work]",

Jewish Wars (Book 1, Preface, Paragraph 1) (1:3) and continuing,

"I thought it therefore an absurd thing to see the truth falsified in affairs of such great consequence, and to take no notice of it; but to suffer those Greeks and Romans that were not in the wars to be ignorant of these things, and to read either flatteries or fictions, 'while the Parthians, and the Babylonians, and the remotest Arabians, and those of our nation beyond Euphrates, with the Adiabeni, by my means, knew accurately both whence the war begun, what miseries it brought upon us, and after what manner it ended'."

Jewish Wars (Book 1 Preface, Paragraph 2) (1:6)

This writer finds it absolutely astounding that for over 50 years, he was taught the scriptures were originally written in the Greek language, and then translated over the centuries into hundreds and hundreds of different tongues. The English scriptures in the 1300's were translated by John Wycliffe. To this date, to his knowledge there is not one Christian College or Seminary anywhere in the world which teaches the Aramaic scriptures as the original first Bible., The English translation came in the 1300's by John Wycliffe and those following including our time honored A.V. K.J.V. 1611 etc. (Even though the 1611 A.V. has some obscurities, and some small parts needing clarification by the ancient languages, this author has grown to love and appreciate it, and probably will use it until death.)

Certainly it was a monumental discovery, one day, when in the Thompson Chain Reference Bible (in my humble opinion the finest Bible reference work in the world) I discovered something on page 181, something that I had never before seen, or knew. There toward the bottom of the stack of historical translations etc, (of course the 'Original Manuscripts' first at the bottom) was the illustration of the 'Most ancient copies' which are clearly identified under the 'Ancient Versions' and under 'c' as… The Peshito or Syriac. The whole Bible date uncertain, (first or second century? Apparently a translation into the common language of certain portions of Syria. What a discovery! I have used the Thompson Bible for years and years, and never had noticed that indeed there were complete Bibles in existence in the world which could be traced to the first or second century A.D.! The eastern Aramaic Peshitta Syrian Bible! The simple fact is that there is not one, no not one complete Greek N.T. from the first or second century, which emphatically shows that God did indeed preserve His Holy Word in the Aramaic Peshitta!! While the Greek translations which went out in the first and second century were honored by God, they were not as clear as to the Deity of our Lord Jesus/Yeshua as the original Aramaic Peshitta was/is. (We have explained later in this booklet concerning the fact while the Tetragrammaton was not translatable from the Hebrew into the Aramaic so 'Yah' Aramaic short for Yahweh or Almighty God was used in its place. It must also be remembered that 'Yah' in Aramaic is identical to the Hebrew Tetragrammaton, YHVH. Then when the scriptures were translated by the apostles into Greek immediately after they were originally penned, the closest words in Greek for Almighty God was 'Kurios or Theos' both used for "Lord or God." The problem with 'Kurios' was that it was also used for Lord as 'lord of a province or country. Of course leave it to the Watchtower to jump on that small weakness of translation, and proclaim that 'Yes Jesus was 'lord' (or 'master') but not LORD in a Deity sense. Much more on this later.)

Bible Persecution by Diocletian

It is quite interesting that as far as this author knows, before Diocletian and Galerius there never was a persecution of the Jews which involved 'burning of sacred scripture' by the powers which ruled over them. Nonetheless, for the first two centuries of the Christian era, no emperor issued general laws against the Christian faith or it's Church. Of course there were some persecutions that did take place (1-2 A.D.) upon the Christians but were carried out under the authority of local government officials. When Emperor Nero executed Christians for their alleged involvement in the fire of 64. This persecution was purely local affair; it did not spread beyond the city limits of Rome. These early persecutions were certainly violent, but they were sporadic, brief and limited in extent. They were of limited threat to Christianity as a whole. The very capriciousness of official action, however, made the threat of state coercion loom large in the Christian imagination. (Wikipedia).

As a nation, the Jews held the O.T. Hebrew Tanakh to be the inspired Word of God. "The Hebrew Bible or Tanakh, is the canonical collection of Hebrew scriptures, including the Torah. These texts are almost exclusively in Biblical Hebrew, with a few passages in Biblical Aramaic." (Wikipedia). Under Roman Rule, the Jews at first seemed to have relatively freedom of worship. However when Diocletian came to rule in end of the third century, he became suspicious of the Jews fearing they could capture the heart and soul of his citizens and turn them away from the Roman gods he worshipped (he and his citizenry). It is claimed that Galerius instigated the coming persecution.

Some (Not Official 1-2 A.D.) Christian Persecution

From its first appearance to its legalization under Constantine, Christianity was an illegal religion in the eyes of the Roman state. For the first two centuries of its existence, Christianity and its practitioners were unpopular with the people at large. Christians were always suspect, members of a "secret society" whose members communicated with a private code and who shied away from the public sphere. It was popular hostility—the anger of the crowd—which drove the earliest persecutions, not official action. Around 112, the governor of Bithynia–Pontus, Pliny, was sent long lists of denunciations of Christians by anonymous citizens, which Emperor Trajan advised him to ignore. In Lyon in 177, it was only the intervention of civil authorities that stopped a pagan mob from dragging Christians from their houses and beating them to death.

To the followers of the traditional cults, Christians were odd creatures: not quite Roman, but not quite barbarian either. Their practices were deeply threatening to traditional mores. Christians rejected public festivals, refused to take part in the imperial cult, avoided public office, and publicly criticized ancient traditions. Conversions tore families apart: Justin Martyr tells of a pagan husband who denounced his Christian wife, and Tertullian tells of children disinherited for becoming Christians. Traditional Roman religion was inextricably interwoven into the fabric of Roman society and state, but Christians refused to observe its practices. In the words of Tacitus, Christians showed "hatred of the human race" (odium generis humani). Among the more credulous, Christians were thought to use black magic in pursuit of revolutionary aims, and to practice incest and cannibalism.

Nonetheless, for the first two centuries of the Christian era, no emperor issued general laws against the faith or it's Church. These persecutions were carried out under the authority of local government officials (Wikipedia).

Christianity, in spite of Roman emperors, Roman prisons, and Roman executions, pursued its silent steady course. In little more than seventy years after the death of Christ, it had made such rapid progress in some places as to threaten the downfall of paganism. The heathen temples were deserted, the worship of the gods was neglected, and victims for sacrifices were rarely purchased. This naturally raised a popular cry against Christianity, such as we had at Ephesus: "This our craft is in danger to be set at naught, and the temple of the great goddess Diana to be despised." Those whose livelihood depended on the worship of the heathen deities, laid many and grievous complaints against the Christians before the governors. This was especially so in the Asiatic provinces where Christianity was most prevalent. (bible-truthpublishers.com

Chapter Three

TO DESTROY THE PESHITTA BLOODY PERSECUTION

Diocletian/Constantine and the Last Persecution of the Church

At the urging of the Caesar Galerius, in 303 Diocletian began the last major persecution of Christians in the Roman Empire resulting in the destruction of churches and the torture and execution of Christians who refused to sacrifice to the Roman gods. God's providence gave us the 27 book New Testament Canon, not the church. God, not men decided the canon.

This providence does not mean that church leaders were inspired in their selecting the canon, only that God had his eye on the scriptures the whole time and brought about His will to form the Bible we see today! Constantine appeared on the scene in the midst of the so-called Great Persecution, begun in 303, under Emperor Diocletian. By 305, the problems caused by the persecution were overtaken by those of determining Diocletian's successor. More than six different generals would fight to become next the emperor. Constantine stood out because he became a Christian and unabashedly made Jesus the patron of his army. By 313, just two contenders remained, Constantine and Licinius. The two jointly issued the Edict of Milan, which made Christianity a legal religion and officially ended the persecution. But, it was not until 324 that Constantine finally became the sole ruler of the Roman Empire.

There are those who blame Constantine, namely the Seventh Day Adventists, for 'changing' the Sabbath to Sunday in 321 A.D. The information as follows clears up this misunderstanding.

In the year 321 A.D., Constantine decreed, "On the venerable day of the Sun let the magistrates and people residing in cities rest, and let all workshops be closed" (Codex Justinianus lib. 3, tit. 12, 3; trans. in Philip Schaff, History of the Christian Church, Vol. 3, p. 380, note 1). Constantine seems to have made this change himself and not through the papacy, since the papacy had not really come in to being at that time. The papacy grew gradually out of the office of Bishop and for many years this was centered in Rome. In any case, it should be noted that in doing this, Constantine is not changing the Sabbath; he is merely making Sunday the official day of rest for the Roman Empire. His motivation was probably not born out of hatred for the Jews (it's hard to say for sure why Constantine or any historical figure did what they did) but out of a desire to adopt what the Christians had practiced for nearly two and a half centuries.

It is well documented that the early church adopted Sunday as their day of worship. Acts 20:7 speaks of this, "On the first day of the week we came together to break bread. Paul spoke to the people …" and 1 Corinthians 16:2, "On the first day of every week, each one of you should set aside a sum of money in keeping with his income, saving it up, so that when I come no collections will have to be made." These passages indicate that Christians were probably meeting regularly on Sunday (the first day of the week). They did this most likely because Christ rose on the first day of the week. It wasn't until hundreds of years later that the death of Christ became the focal point of Christian worship services. That is not to say they thought it unimportant; but they were primarily concerned with His victory over death realized in His resurrection. (Quotation from web site, gotquestions.org)

Constantine saw Christianity's belief in one god as a way to unify the empire that had been so badly divided for two decades. But he discovered that Christianity itself was not unified. So, he called the Council of Nicea in 325 to bring together the 1,800 bishops from around the empire to work out official doctrine and provide the basis for a unified Church. ...The council laid the foundation of orthodox theology (Catholic theology) and declared several differing theologies heresies. Constantine's support initially gave Orthodoxy the ability to require Christians to adopt their doctrinal formulation. While during the next few decades, the church's fortunes waxed and waned, within a century, Christianity had been declared the official religion of the Roman Empire and non-Christian religions were in steep decline. (cbaldwin@uwyo.edu UW Religion Today. How Constantine created the Christian {Roman Catholic Ed.}Church.)

So there you have it. Constantine, who was not baptized until his death, no doubt thinking that baptism would be his main key to soon enter the kingdom of God unwittingly endorsed the false doctrine of baptismal regeneration. The very first church in existence was not the Roman Catholic Church. The first one was the church at Jerusalem founded by the disciples of Jesus/Yeshua in the first century. Note the following:

> What marks the beginning of the Christian Church, the social organization uniting Christians? The answer depends on the definition of "church." If "church" means the people who adhere to Jesus' teachings, then Jesus began it. Some Christians believe that Peter founded the church at the behest of Jesus himself. Others (including the author of this booklet) would see the first church as the Jerusalem Church, created by the disciples after Jesus' death and led

by James until his death in 63 A.D. cbaldwin@uwyo.edu UW Religion Today.

Unfortunately we have seen the 'church' which was endorsed and created by marrying it to the state by Constantine, and making it the official religion of the Roman Empire, becoming the Roman Catholic Church of today. Not only that, but the pagan religion of Nimrod bringing along all of its errors, (which dwelt freely in Rome), morphed into his new Roman Church. The true apostolic church, the fundamental true church was not interested in joining with Constantine's new found 'faith,' due to its doctrinal errors. Over the coming centuries it would be greatly persecuted by Pope after Pope. Constantine's state church eventually came up with its own version/translation of the scriptures etc. Then unfortunately for the damnation of countless souls, the Roman (Catholic) Church locked the scriptures into the Latin dialect during the dark ages and forbid the common people to have a copy, and/or to read and understand it for themselves! Even today supposedly the priest is the only one to be able to read, understand and preach the scripture. The apostolic church on the other hand proudly still had the original/copies of the original scriptures, the Aramaic Peshitta, which they hid from burning by Diocletian. Historically only when the state is over and in control of the church is there ever any persecution of the true people of God.

Why the division? Why are there so many of differing theological positions concerning the deity of our Lord Jesus Christ? To some, He was merely a created being, yea an angel which according to the Mormons makes Lucifer His 'spirit' brother before his fall from heaven. (See www.bible.ca/su-deity-christ.htm for full info.) Like Herbert W. Armstrong, the Mormons teach divine progression. Supposedly, Jesus was once just a man who lived on another planet. He eventually progressed to be equal to God and came to colonize planet earth creating or producing humans as «gods to be.»

To those who look upon our Lord Jesus as a created being such as the Watchtower, etc. the following needs to be remembered.

1. An angel as a created being is not a member of the human race of which only a true member of the human race, directly related in lineage to Adam would be qualified to die in man's place for man's sins.

2. That man to qualify to die for sinful man, for his sins, must be sinless, but not capable of sin, thus disqualifying him from being an angel. Angels have proven their ability to commit sin. Remember Lucifer and one third of the angels sinned and fell from heaven. The fact is that God cannot sin, and no possibility of Him sinning which means only one equal to God and still fully man, could qualify to die for man's sins. Jesus/Yeshua being born of the lineage of man, did not have the sinful blood of Adam in his veins, but yea rather His blood was the blood of God! A baby has the blood of his father in his veins. Jesus did not have the sinful blood of Adam flowing in His veins. Acts 20:28. "Take heed therefore unto yourselves, and to all the flock, over the which the Holy Ghost hath made you overseers, to feed the church of God, which He hath purchased with his\His own blood." Only a sinless man who was born into the lineage of man, who was also fully God, could possibly die in our place. Truly Jesus Yeshua was fully God/man!

II Corinthians 5:19&21

To wit, that God was in Christ (Watchtower please note that Almighty God YHVH literally was permanently indwelling the body of Christ, God was IN Christ) reconciling the world unto Himself…etc…For He hath made Him to be sin for us who knew no sin, that we might be made the righteousness of God in Him.

To others (most of traditional historic Christianity) He was literally God incarnate in the flesh, veritably God/Jehovah encased in human flesh, and then according to others such as Muslims etc., He is only a great prophet of God, indeed only a normal man who represented the true God of the heavens, they have erroneously named Allah. Certainly no matter what the theological perspective one may hold concerning Jesus (Aramaic Yeshua to be correct), He was the greatest man who ever walked the face of the earth, and yea even our calendars are set by His coming! B.C. /A.D…

One may ask, "Does it really make a difference if Jesus was really God come in the flesh as long as one holds Him as a true representative of God? To this we must answer an emphatic YES, since His claims were very open and dogmatic to those of His generation, and as also recorded in the Holy text, the New Testament. Our Savior openly claimed to be the only door to heaven, the only way of access to God, yea by Him the only way to receive salvation and eternal life in heaven. Jesus said "I am the door, by me if any man shall enter in he shall be saved, "and also that "…for there is none other name under heaven given among men whereby we must be saved." Acts 4:12. Thus it is plain and simple; the scriptures abundantly teach that outside of our God and Savior the Lord Jesus Christ no one can have redemption or salvation. Certainly if Jesus was not who He claimed to be, would make him a false teacher, guilty of blasphemy.

This author finds it so sad that those who reject the doctrine of the deity of Christ, while they may be sincere and devoutly dedicated to their church or synagogues, such as Mormons, Muslims, Watchtower etc., they will not find salvation or peace with God in this life. It is well to say that the same holds true when one corrupts the Biblical doctrine of salvation by repentance and faith in Christ as the only way to be saved. When one adds to, or takes away from the doctrine of justification by faith and faith alone, they corrupt God's only plan of salvation,

(namely that Jesus is the Savior, not Jesus plus good works, baptism, catechism etc, etc.) and pave their way to a burning fiery Hell!

Salvation lies only in one fact, namely that salvation can only be obtained by simple repentance of one's sin, and then by exercising faith in the Lord Jesus Christ believing that He is very God come in the flesh to redeem us by His shed blood on the cross, giving us eternal redemption from our sins. It is an egregious error to demand baptism, confirmation, church membership, good works etc, to be added into the way to be saved. Only the Lord Jesus Christ is the Savior, not Jesus plus. Thus false religions pervert the way of salvation by adding to it, and close the door of heaven to those seeking to come to salvation. Their faith is corrupted, and rendered incomplete by viewing a false way (false gospel) of salvation paving the way to their path to Hell. Paul emphasized such when he said, "For I am not ashamed of the gospel of Christ for it is the power of God unto salvation..." and again, "If any man preach any other gospel unto you than I have preached, let him be accursed." He plainly said in Corinthians "...for Christ sent me not to baptize but to preach the gospel..."

Yes it does matter what one believes about Jesus, Aramaic Yeshua. Our time honored K.J.V. certainly does deserve the title of the Trinity Bible» as some writers refer to it. What it is important to realize though is that the A.V. 1611 does have obscurity in a number of places in fully explaining the Deity of Christ, where as the Aramaic Eastern Peshitta, (original language which mirrors the autographs) irrefutably gives such truth without weakness, but weakness did come by translation from the Aramaic into the Greek and other languages. One Aramaic scholar, Steve Caruso, (see footnote below) has questioned the Aramaic manuscripts he has examined, and claims that the Aramaic manuscripts he has examined appear to be from later centuries, since they do not mirror some common Aramaic language of the first century.

Brother Bauscher does not hold to Mr. Caruso' just stated view and gives clear reason just why he does not. Note Brother Bauscher's following note:

> **Note:** The above bold type sentence is a false statement. The Aramaic text of the Peshitta NT is preserved in mss. dating back to the 5th century, which is the earliest we can date any Peshitta ms. known today, but all Peshitta mss. (several hundred) are practically identical to each other and are so carefully copied that they are quoted in Syriac by church fathers verbatim in many places in the early 4th century and are held by the Church of the East to be identical to the originals written by the Apostles, and to be copied so carefully throughout their scribal tradition through the centuries that no differences exist between the manuscripts, and even the few minor variations there are can easily be resolved by comparing several mss. together at any one place in the text. "In the mouth of two or three witnesses, every word shall be established." See Deut 17:6; Mat 18:16; John 8:17; 2 Cor 13:1;1 Tim 5:19; Heb. 10:28. A 5th century Peshitta ms. is practically identical to a 15th century ms. , to an 8th century ms., to a 17th century hand copied ms. They just have not changed over 1500 years at all! No Peshitta ms. was translated from Greek. Some other Syriac mss. were, which are called "Harklean". This Harklean version was produced in AD 616. It is <u>very</u> different from Peshitta mss. A 5th century Peshitta ms. would be unchanged and practically identical to a 1st century Peshitta ms. And a 1st century ms. has been discovered and catalogued:

Brother Bauscher further notes the following:

His (Caruso's) description of the Gospels manuscript referenced above is doubtless a Peshitta manuscript, whose original exemplar was dated AD 78. The Maronite Church would have used nothing but a Peshitta manuscript for its church liturgy, readings and homilies in the 18 th century and prior.

There is a lot of controversy about which New Testament manuscripts are the closest to the original manuscripts, but there is no known manuscript with an actual date on it which assures it was actually written in the first century, except this one of the Gospels which is noticed, cited and translated by Giuseppe Assemani in 1728.

The specificity of the citation is compelling, inspiring the trust of the reader that the scribe who wrote it was testifying to the day, month and year of the writing of the manuscript -(AD 78 in a traditional 1 st century date method using 311 BC as a starting point). He also named the copyist as "Akhay, fellow Apostle Mar Maray, the disciple of Addai, who was the Apostle"(of Jesus)!

But I am not surprised. I have seen many other evidences that the Peshitta was not only written in the first century, but that it is the original God written New Testament. They will be forthcoming. For now, I can say that the very best evidence I know is the Peshitta itself. If you read it and compare it to other New Testaments, either the Aramaic text itself, or a good translation of it, you will see and hear the divinity of its words, if you read it with your heart and mind in The Spirit by whom it was written. I will go even a step further and say, if you read the Peshitta in The Spirit by whom it was written, you will hear, not only the words, but the very voice of God. "End Bauscher comment".

It is of utmost importance to remember the fact that the New Testament was originally written in Aramaic, the language of Yeshua and His disciples. It is a fact also that in translation of any material religious or otherwise the impact of certain truths are lost to some lesser or greater degree. This now brings us to the doctrine of 'verbal plenary inspiration' or better yet 'verbal plenary preservation,' which is a doctrine which cannot be compromised, or shortchanged in even the slightest degree. A very simple explanation of this doctrine is as follows: (Biblical inspiration - Wikipedia)

Verbal plenary inspiration: This view gives a greater role to the human writers of the Bible while maintaining a belief that God preserved the integrity of the words of the Bible The effect of Bible inspiration was to move the authors so as to produce the words God wanted.

Then there is the view of 'verbal dictation' inspiration of the Word of God which is as follows:

Verbal dictation describes a theory about how the Holy Spirit was involved with the people who first physically inscribed the Bible. According to this theory, the human role was a purely mechanical one: their individuality was by-passed whilst they wrote, and neither did their cultural background have any influence on what they wrote, because these writers were under the control of God. This may have been the original understanding of inspiration for the people of the Bible.

According to James Barr this theory of inspiration was popular among Protestant theologians during the sixteenth and seventeenth centuries. According to Frederic Farrar, Martin Luther did not understand inspiration to mean that scripture was dictated in a purely mechanical manner. Instead, Luther «held that they were not dictated by the Holy Spirit, but that His illumination produced in the minds of their writers the knowledge of salvation, so that divine truth had been expressed in human form, and the knowledge of God had become a personal possession of man. The actual writing was a human not a supernatural act. Farrar says that John Calvin also rejected the verbal dictation theory. Today, according to T.D. Lea and H.P. Griffen, respected evangelicals maintain that God dictated the words of Scripture.

There of course are many attacks upon the idea that God gave words to man, for man to write them down for future ('commoners' i.e. non-clergy) posterities edification and salvation. One such attack on that truth is well known in church history found in the Roman

Catholic Church and their demand for only the priest to be the one to 'interpret' the Bible to parishioners, that only they are qualified and suited to understand God's message to man. A very clear example of such is found in the article by "Official Website of The Catholic Diocese Of Little Rock," Jan. 12, 2002 as follows: (Quoting)

"The most important norm in Catholic interpretation is the authentic tradition of the Church. The Bible was given to the believing community of Jesus' disciples, not to individuals, and only the community, acting under the Spirit's guidance through its appointed leaders, is empowered to define its teaching. The contemporary Church reads the Bible in the context of the tradition of interpretation through the centuries in order to locate the constants." End.

> **(Readers note) Steve Caruso (MLIS)** has translated Aramaic languages professionally for over 15 years with a focus upon the Galilean dialect – the language spoken by Jesus of Nazareth. He is presently the Program Coordinator for Interface Design & Web Development at Raritan Valley Community College. (End).

How plain it is to see the fallacy of such thinking. Following is the Catholic progression of thought in understanding what God says (to their parishioners) in the Bible:

1. The Bible was given to the disciples of Christ, not to individuals.

2. The appointed leaders over the disciples, alone are guided by the Spirit to understand/define the Bible to (leaders in this case the Catholic church hierarchy/leaders) the disciples..

3. The disciples in turn are empowered therefore under the appointed leaders to define Biblical truth.

4. Then the contemporary Church is to understand the Bible in the doctrines of traditional Roman Catholic Church historical interpretation in order to find the constants.

So there you have it. Roman Catholic Church tradition from thousands of years of previous history is the deciding criteria (?) of what God meant (for Catholics when they are being schooled) when He gave us His Word! In plain English, that simply means, "Don't believe what the Scriptures say to you, but rather allow the Roman Catholic Church to tell you what they mean in the light of our historical infallibility (?!). Some may ignorantly ask, "So what is wrong with that, since the church surely wouldn't lead us astray?" The answer to that is simple. Then the Bible does not mean what it says, nor does it say what it means, and is therefore open to whatever interpretation is assigned to it by the theological position of the church in ages past. This includes whatever dogmas they desire to impart to parishioners even if it contradicts the Bible. God's Word is therefore subjugated to whatever the church held/holds it to mean, based on what tradition from centuries past defined it to mean!

The real problem with this Catholic position on understanding the Bible is rather than let the Bible speak to us as it is written, they can make the Word of God mean whatever they wish it to mean. Secondly they can keep their parishioners enslaved to any false doctrine(s) they may hold, by forbidding a searching soul to read the Bible and understand it for themselves. Now this discussion about the 'meaning' of scripture leads to the paramount importance of the God breathed and perfect transmission of God's word to us! Whether the transmission from the Spirit of God of God's word to us was infallibly perfect or not, and that perfection was not affected by the human scribe element cannot be questioned.

II Timothy 3:16

> For all scripture is given by inspiration of God and is profitable for doctrine, for reproof, for correction for instruction in righteousness.

II Peter 1:21

>For prophecy never came by the will of man, but holy men of God spoke as they were moved by the Holy Spirit.

Now in this author's opinion, it matters not whether the scriptures were of verbal dictation, or verbal plenary inspiration so long as it is understood that the scriptures coming from the God inspired pens of the writers were 100% exactly as God wanted them, down to the smallest jot or tittle. Nevertheless there remains one huge problem for the church. That problem is as follows. If we are to believe that the autographs (New Testament original documents) were absolutely without the slightest error, and were 100% perfectly given to us under the inspiration of the Spirit of God, (there can be no doubt that such is/was the case), then of the thousands of ancient manuscripts which all have some variation from the others, to some degree how do we know what is the closest Testament to the originals?

Consider the Siniatic, Vaticanus, Alexendrian manuscripts which date back from 350-450 a.d., also the over 2k Greek manuscripts called the Received Text/Byzentine Text/Textus Receptus, the basis of the time honored A.V. 1611 K.J.V. That also must include the secondary Aramaic New Testament copies of the originals from the second century or so (secondary since they were no doubt copied from the original Aramaic sacred texts or copies of the same), which manuscripts have a completeness which no other lineage can point to. Even the Latin manuscripts must be included along with some others which no doubt were copies of copies of the originals, or copies of copies of copies of the originals.

So… following are some subjects of interest who supposedly received God's message for the world separate from the Old and New Testaments

1. Mary Baker Eddy, founder of 'Christian Science' with her 'Science and Health With key to the Scriptures.' Supposedly given to her by the inspired hand of God.

2. Joseph Smith, founder of the Mormon movement and his 'Book of Mormon' supposedly written on golden tablets provided by the angel Moroni which was supposed to be the perfect word of God for his new movement.

3. The Prophet Mohammed, founder of Islam with the Koran. According to conventional Islamic belief, the Koran was supposedly revealed by the angel Gabriel to the Prophet Muhammad in the West Arabian towns Mecca and Medina beginning in 610 and ending with Muhammad's death in 632 A.D. Those in Islam consider the Koran the perfect inspired Holy book of God.

4. Peter Ruckman. Ruckman holds (held, he has passed away) that the A.V. 1611 K.J.V. Bible was 100% perfectly translated under the direct superintendence of the Spirit of God for the world today, in the English language. As well he claims the over 200 minor translation differences (?) are in fact new and Divine revelations which were not in the original manuscripts. (It is here important for this author myself, to verify that I do indeed view the family of manuscripts commonly known as the 'Textus Receptus' (direct descendants from the original God breathed Aramaic MS.) which was the basis for the K.J.V. as being correctly called the Word of God, though there are places in the text which may need clarification from the older manuscripts.)

There is no doubt that even though there are many many slight variations in all of these manuscripts, there are no variations which would/could be said to be guilty of perverting or corrupting any cardinal fundamental essential doctrine of God's Word! Considering all of this, the problem still looms, "Where is the Word of God in its original perfection, yea in such perfection that we can use it to judge any extant manuscript, whether Greek, Aramaic, Latin or English, etc, etc?" The monstrous Ruckman heresy claims that the true Word of God in all of its majesty, infallibility was reintroduced to the world in the 1611 A.V. K.J.V. as it was translated under the supposedly divinely 'superintended' 'Spirit of God perfectly inspired translation done by King James translators. (Readers note: It is hoped that this booklet will reintroduce the truth held in the Eastern Aramaic Peshitta.)

The Ruckmanites (they prefer to be called 'Ruckman Knights) are thereby able to falsely conclude that this 1611 translation was superior to the manuscripts from which it was taken and can even correct them!? As well, while we all should know that there are definitely some corrupted ancient manuscripts, he claims that ALL (present or past) versions are 'Of the devil.' Thankfully, thanks to Glenn David Bauscher's monumental discovery of the original Bible the final nail has been placed into the coffin of Peter S. Ruckman's heresies! Go to aramaicnt.net to find the original restored Aramaic Peshitta Bible as it was originally given to the disciples under Divine inspiration. A true miracle in itself thanks to Rev. Bauscher). No doubt, Rev. Baushcher's perfectly restored Peshitta Aramaic manuscript is an identical replica of the original Word of God given by Divine inspiration through the apostles in the first century. Truly the most important discovery in 2000 or so years of church history!! Equally important the manuscript can be positively mathematically proven to be infallibly perfect due to the underlying codes found in the text. Absolutely no other manuscript in history has such mathematically provable codes in the text.

It is well to pause here, to further expose Ruckmanism for what it is. Ruckman has built a flourishing ministry in Florida by claiming that he and he alone has discovered over 200 (?) advanced revelations divinely incorporated into the 1611 A.V. King James version Bible, which were not in the original manuscripts. We will attempt to only touch on the smallest basic heresies he holds. (This author (myself), believes that God has a very uncomfortable 'special place' in the next world for him and people like Hyles. Perhaps they can give each other some kind of consolation.)

Chapter Four

PETER RUCKMAN FALSE APOSTLE-FALSE PROPHET

In all of church history there has never been anyone who has made the outlandish claims concerning the 1611 K.J.V. that Ruckman has made, saying that the pure and complete word of God was not available to the world until the year 1611, since the original autographs, O.T. and N.T. simply disappeared due to age etc., and as well the extant Greek (etc) manuscripts were not accurate enough to be reliable. I.e. he falsely claims that God did not give us a complete Bible in the first century under inspiration of the Holy Spirit. So…the supposed added revelations were discovered by him and him alone for his followers.

1. Ruckman claims that the English Bible of 1611 is as a translation 100% accurate and infallibly correct in its entirety. He also claims that the A.V. contains many 'advanced revelations' that the original autographs do not have. Quoting from his "Bible Believers Bulletin" as follows: "It is late at night, kiddies. Time for bye-bye. There are more than forty-five advanced revelations in a King James Bible that no Hebrew or Greek scholar was able to find in any set of Greek manu-

scripts, in any translation of any Hebrew text, for any version in any language, published by anyone who rejected the AV as the final and infallible authority. (Ruckman, Peter. Bible Believers' Bulletin. Dec. 2005, p. 13) We quote as follows: "If you are able to obtain a copy [Ruckman's proposed new book] you will have, in your hands, a minimum of 200 advanced revelations that came from the inerrant English text, that were completely overlooked (or ignored) by every major Christian scholar since 90 A.D." (Bible Believers' Bulletin, Jan. 1994, pp. 2, 4).

2. Thus he has brought upon himself the curse of Revelation which plainly warns against adding to, or taking away from the Word of God.

3. He has shown absolutely no literary or researchable iron clad facts as to the above claims, but his attitude is, "…the above are true because I say it is.

4. Absolutely not one scholar, who knows the original languages, would dare make such claims such as he has made.

5. Ruckman forgot that the 1611 A.V. is/was a translation of ancient manuscripts and then outrageously claims that the A.V. 1611 English Bible can correct ANY current or previous Hebrew/Aramaic/Greek/English (etc) manuscript or for that matter any manuscript or Bible translation that exists or has ever existed. (Of course any fundamental Bible believing Christian believes the family of the Textus Receptus brings us the infallible Word of God insofar as such is accurate in its translation. It is just a simple fact that some translations are better than others, while many times there is a need to go to the original languages for a clearer understanding/clarification of what is written.)

6. Ruckman's above claims therefore teaches that God gave us an inferior Bible or better stated God gave us inferior original autographs that were not the perfect God breathed text thus contradicting 2 Tim. 3:16. "…All scripture is given by inspiration of God…"

7. Ruckman describes a UFO descending and bringing the anti-Christ to earth, and as well he does not consider aborting a fetus as murder!

8. Ruckmanism is in reality, a subtle satanic attack upon the holy Word of God. By him pontificating his supposed 'advanced revelations' (which are not in the original manuscripts) he becomes guilty of adding to the Word of God, which automatically makes him a confirmed liar. The book of Revelation places a certain curse upon anyone who adds to or takes away from the Word of God. This author, myself, therefore cannot believe Ruckman was a regenerated truly born again child of God making such claim with his blasphemy.

9. Ruckman teaches that the Word of God can be changed from century to century and yet still be infallible and inerrant! (See Ruckman, Peter. **Greek Manuscript Evidence**. Pensacola, FL: Bible Baptist Bookstore, circa 1970's. CD audio recording, about 30-32 minutes into track 4). The fact is that the K.J.V. was not translated under the inspiration of the Spirit of God. If one will but read the original preface to the original 1611 A.V. the translators readily admitted what they were undertaking was just that, a translation, nothing more, nothing less! Interesting it is, that this original preface destroys the K.J.O. (King James only cult/and Ruckmanism) position that all translations or versions before or after the A.V. 1611

are of Satanic origin. The original 1611 A.V. preface certainly is an embarrassment to them.

Detroit Baptist Theological Seminary has commented on the original preface to the K.J.V. 1611 quote following: " This preface is primarily a defense of the new translation, but it also provides important information about the translators' views on the subject of Bible translation. It is an embarrassment (or should be) to King James-only advocates because it contains statements from the translators that are in direct opposition to the KJV-only position. It is most unfortunate that this preface is no longer included in modern copies of the KJV."

Next there follows a long section praising Scripture, noting its great value and divine origin. But the perfections of Scripture can never be appreciated unless it is understood, and it cannot be understood until it is translated into the common tongue. Translation is therefore a good thing. Thus, God in his providence raised up individuals to translate the Old Testament into Greek. The Septuagint, though far from perfect, was still sufficient as the Word of God, such that the apostles quoted it in the NT. And even thought the Septuagint was the Word of God, scholars believed it could be improved, which led to the Greek versions of Aquila, Theodotion, and Symmachus, as well as the Hexapla of Origen.

 Both testaments were then translated into Latin, culminating in Jerome's Vulgate. Finally, the Scriptures were translated into many tongues, including English. However, the preface observes, the Roman Catholic Church has generally not allowed the Scriptures to be rendered into the common tongues. Recently, they have produced their own translation of the Bible into English though they seem to have been forced to do it against their better judgment due to the number of Protestant English Bibles available.

The preface then returns to the problem of opposition to the new translation, and translations in general, by answering several objections. The main argument against the new translation questions the need for it, that is, since there had already been a number of English translations of the Bible, why is there need for another? If previous translations were good, there should be no need for another; if they were defective, why were they ever offered in the first place? The answer is, of course, that "nothing is begun and perfected at the same time." While the efforts of previous English translators are to be commended, nevertheless, they themselves, if they were alive, would thank the translators of this new translation. The previous English Bibles were basically sound, but this new translation affords an opportunity to make translation improvements and needed clarifications.

The translators argue that all previous English translations can rightly be called the Word of God, even though they may contain some "imperfections and blemishes." Just as the King's speech which he utters in Parliament is **still the King's speech**, though it may be imperfectly translated into French, Dutch, Italian, and Latin; so also in the case of the translation of the Word of God. For translations will never be infallible since they are not like the original manuscripts, which were produced by the apostles and their associates under the influence of inspiration. However, even an imperfect translation like the Septuagint can surely be called the Word of God since it was approved and used by the apostles themselves.

But since all translations are imperfect, the Church of Rome should not object to the continual process of correcting and improving English translations of the Bible. Even their own Vulgate has gone through many revisions since the day of Jerome.

Finally, the translators state the purpose and plan of the present translation. They have not intended to make a new translation, but to make the best possible translation by improving upon previous ones.

To do so they have, of course, carefully examined the original Hebrew and Greek since translation should only be done from the original tongues. Also, they did not work hastily, as did the translators of the Septuagint, who, according to legend, finished their work in only seventy-two days. The translators also availed themselves of commentaries and translations of the Scriptures in other languages. In their work they felt it was essential to include marginal notes, despite the fact that some might feel such notes tend to undermine the authority of the Scriptures.

These notes are essential since the translators confess that oftentimes they were unsure how a word or phrase should be translated. This is especially true in Hebrew, where there are a number of words which only occur once in Scripture, and even the Jews themselves are uncertain about their translation. And so, as Augustine notes, a "variety of translations is profitable for finding out of the sense of the Scriptures." Lastly, the translators observe that, in spite of criticism from some quarters, they decided not to always translate the same Hebrew or Greek word with the same English word and have retained, over the objections of the Puritans, the old ecclesiastical words like "baptism" instead of "washings."

It must be considered that when a perfectly honest person conveys a written message, that message must contain the following:

1. A message or statement which exactly and perfectly represents what message is in that person's mind.
2. That message cannot have any errors or misrepresentations at all in the text from the hand of the scribe or from the one making the message into print.

3. That message must have an indelible imprint somewhere somehow within it, to prove that it originated from its author, and therefore it cannot be altered, or counterfeited.

How refreshing it is, therefore that finally in this century, Rev. Glenn David Bauscher has managed to achieve restoring for the church the original Bible, exactly as it came from the New Testament writers pens! It need be said that it is not the intention of this book to improve upon, or expand Rev. Baushcer's findings, but rather to use them to give perfect examples of how the Aramaic Bible is so crystal clear so as to irrefutably prove Jesus is/was Jehovah YHWH come in the flesh in the person of our Lord Jesus Christ. Next we must look into the Tetragrammaton and the error it exposes in the Watchtower (erroneously and irreverently called Jehovah Witnesses.) Interestingly enough, another very vital truth comes to light here concerning the Tetragrammaton and the original Aramaic New Testament, that being the fact that the original N.T. given in the Aramaic, is much more clear than the Greek, in irrefutably proving that the Lord Jesus Christ was YHWH come in the flesh! But first:

The Ruckmanite Attack Upon the Original Word of the Lord the Wonderful Inerrant Eastern Original Restored Aramaic Peshitta
The Ruckman heresy is a subtle Satanic attack upon the original Bible! How so some say? Simple. There was one and only one original 100% letter perfect word for word Divinely inspired group of N.T. manuscripts given to the world in the first century a.d. That group of manuscripts was the Aramaic Peshitta manuscripts penned by the apostles those holy men of God who spoke as they were moved by the Holy Spirit! To think that God would give us such a wonderful gift in A.D.1 and then allow it to be destroyed or corrupted beyond inerrancy (by satanic powers) for future generations to be deprived of the exacting truths God desired to impart to His people, is not conceivable!! When this author was in college, a friend (Ruckmanite if my memory serves

me correctly), went to Professor Peter Connolly (an elderly theology professor) and asked him (accusingly of course) "So if the K.J.V. is not 100% perfect and sometimes needs be clarified by the Greek, then where is the true Word of God in this world?" To that question Dr. Connolly waved his arm across the wall in his office where hundreds of theological books stood and said, "The Word of God is there."

Ruckman very subtly has used the gross ignorance of the traditional Christian church of the Peshitta Aramaic New Testament to lead Christians into believing the A.V. 1611 K.J.V. is what God intends to take place of the original manuscripts. Then by claiming over two hundred so called advanced revelations in the A.V. he insinuates that the original manuscripts were not God's complete perfect revelation to us! That plainly is a lie. While the K.J.V is a time honored translation of the Word of God, it is just that, a translation, nothing more and nothing less. This author uses it every day, and probably will till he goes to be with the LORD.

The simple fact is that there is at present one and only one sacred perfect family (of course including the Hebrew O.T.) of manuscripts in the world, and that is the Eastern Aramaic Peshitta New Testament, restored by the Rev. Glenn David Bauscher, whose web site is aramaicnt.net. A miracle indeed that can be scientifically tried tested and proven. The underlying Divine codes in the text, watermarks if you will, irrefutably prove that only Godly men under Divine inspiration of the Spirit of God, could have possibly penned it.

Ruckman Admitting to Being Regularly Demon Posessed

Astonishing as it is, Ruckman in the following utube, claims that he at times, or sometimes whenever, becomes possessed with a demon or demons, and needs to cast them out, which he does by standing in front of a mirror, and commanding them to depart in the name of Jesus. https://www.youtube.com/watch?v=PLQlQFDMSsg (starting at 3:20)

Now for any true blood washed, born again Christian to claim to be (regularly/often etc.,) demon possessed needing to be exorcised is contrary to the Bible the Word of God. It must be remembered that a truly born again Christian has the Holy Spirit of God/Christ indwelling his body. That the Holy Spirit is sealed there, living there will be there until the day of redemption and no demon, can indwell the temple of God which is our bodies. (I Cor. 3:16-17, and Eph. 4:30). To this author, this is proof positive that Ruckman is really unsaved, or a demonically possessed heretic. Enough on Ruckman

Chapter Five

The Precious Invaluable Tetragrammaton the Tetragrammaton

YHWH or YHVH are the consonants used in the Old Testament Hebrew manuscripts specifically in reference to the Lord of heaven the God of Israel. One definition of this word is given as follows:

> What is the **Tetragrammaton?**" Answer: The ancient Hebrew language that the Old **Testament** was written in did not have vowels in its alphabet. In written form, ancient Hebrew was a consonant-only language. In the original Hebrew, God's name transliterates to YHWH (sometimes written in the older style as JHVH), referring to the God of Israel. Quotation from:

What is YHWH? What is the Tetragrammaton? | GotQuestions.org
www.gotquestions.org/YHWH-Tetragrammaton.html

This title commonly refers to God, or Lord, by the Hebrews, and was a title which was held *so sacred, that the Jews would refuse to speak it.* Pronunciation: In written form, ancient Hebrew was a consonant-only language without any vowels, thus leading to the reference to the God of Israel being spelled "YHWH, or JHVH." Because of this, *the word itself gives no indication of actual pronunciation. This issue is compounded because of a Jewish taboo on speaking God's name.* Another interesting explanation of these four consonants is as follows:

The **Tetragrammaton**, referred to in rabbinic literature as HaShem (The Name) or Shem Hameforash (The Special Name), is the word used to refer to the four-letter word, yud-hey-vav-hey (הוהי), that is the reference (not name) to or for God used in the Hebrew Bible. (Read from right to left). Quotation from: What Is The Tetragrammaton? www.myjewishlearning.com.

So...just what errors have come to light concerning the Watchtower and the Tetragrammaton? Well first, comes the problem with the truly correct pronunciation of the four consonants. Then secondly the problem comes when the Greek translations of the Aramaic in the first century had no linguistic ability to use the four consonants, so rather used the Greek "Kurios and Theos" as the terms to be translated as LORD, Lord, lord, God and god! As well, the common (Aramaic) term for Israel's God, was MarYah, which is a combination of two Aramaic terms 'Mar or <u>Lord</u>,' with '<u>Yah'</u> which is the accepted Aramaic shortened form of YHVH. Ancient Jews often called God "Elohim" which is plural, or "Eloha" which is singular. The Aramaic people often called God "Alaha" which is the equivalent of the Hebrew "Eloha." Thus began a slight step down translating from the original Aramaic into the Greek, in not so clearly identifying the Lord Jesus Christ, and just who He really was. Was He just a good man, or an honorable prophet speaking for and representing God? Or was He a created being, created by Elohim before the world was made, created as an angelic being making Him Lucifers brother? Or was He literally God Almighty, the second person of the Trinity, coming down from heaven, forming Himself a human body in which to permanently live, and literally becoming "God Man?" Interesting it is that the Watchtower correctly point out that the Tetragramaton was used by the first century and earlier Jews to identify the God of Israel. They then incorrectly surmise that the *Greek* manuscripts which, they (erroneously) assume were the originals, had to have had the Tetragrammaton when they refer to the Almighty God, the God of Israel. Yes the original autographs did indeed have the Tetragrammaton (no not as YHWH) but the Aramaic substitute equal 'Yah" (short form of YHVH) included when referring to the Almighty, *but the originals (autographs penned by the apostles) were in the Aramaic language and not in the Greek!*

The Tetragrammaton certainly was the reference to all the world, that it referred to Him and Him alone, the Almighty and only true God! The Watchtower has overlooked irrefutable scripture reference as to exactly what the 'name' of the Almighty really is. Following is the conversation between Moses and the Lord at the burning bush experience, as the Lord was commissioning Moses to face Pharaoh to release the children of Israel:

Exodus 3:13-15

And Moses said unto God, Behold, when I come unto the children of Israel, and shall say unto them, The God of your fathers hath sent me unto you and they shall say to me, What is His name? What shall I say unto them? And God said unto Moses, *I AM THAT I AM* sent me unto you. And God said moreover unto Moses, Thus shalt thou say unto **the children of Israel The Lord God of your fathers the God of Abraham, the God of Isaac, and the God of Jacob hath sent me unto you.** *This is my name forever and this is my memorial unto all generations."*

Following is a clear explanation of the above verses from the original by Hebrew scholar Roy Reinhold

Mr. Reinhold explains that the eternal memorial name of God is the Tetragrammaton/YHVH/JHVH. Yahweh which in Hebrew is vud hed vav hey which was not correctly translated into the English A.V. It should have been Yahweh. This is evident in Exodus 3:13-15 which was erroneously translated as "I am that I am." Further he explains that it should also read "And Elohim said more to Moses…and you shall say to the Israelites Yahweh…the God of your fathers…He has sent me to you this is His name forever…this is how I will be remembered…"

Next our Lord freely uses the 'I AM' title of deity for Himself

John 8: 57-59

> Then said the Jews unto him, Thou art not yet fifty years old, and hast thou seen Abraham? Jesus said unto them, Verily verily I say unto you, before Abraham was "I AM." Then took they up stones to cast at him, but Jesus hid himself…

Here, not only was He proclaiming His pre-existence to Abraham, but as well was proclaiming that He was the 'I AM" or the same one who appeared to Moses as the God of Israel at the burning bush! The Jews (well knowing the Hebrew Old Testament) did not take up stones to stone him for claiming pre-existence to Abraham, but because He was claiming to be one and the same as God! Which He was! I.e. God come in the form of a man! Clearly as well in Isaiah the Messiah was identified as God come in the form of a man:

Isaiah 9:6

> "For unto us a child is born, unto us a son is given: and the government shall be upon his shoulder: and his name shall be called Wonderful, Counselor, The Mighty God, the everlasting Father, Prince of Peace…" and then again in:

John 1: 1 & 14

"In the beginning was the Word, and the Word was with God, and the Word was God...And the Word was made flesh and dwelt among us..."

Sad it is that the Watchtower translation has added the unwarranted definite article "a" into John 1:1 making Jesus a lesser 'god.' The originals do not support such addition. And then again in...

1 Tim. 3:16

"And without controversy, great is the mystery of godliness: God was manifest in the flesh, justified in the Spirit, seen of angels, preached unto the Gentiles, believed on in the world, received up into glory." And again when appearing to Thomas:

John 20: 27-29

"...be not faithless but believing (Jesus said). And Thomas answered and said unto Him, My Lord and my God! Jesus said unto him, Thomas because thou hast seen me thou hast believed." Lastly note:

Col. 2:8

"For in Him dwelleth all the fullness of the Godhead bodily."

How clear it is here in the scripture that in the body of our Savior, the Godhead in its entirety dwelt! Yeshua certainly was literally God come in the flesh in the form of man.

Comment from "Treasury of Scripture Knowledge" as follows:

"I am." That our Lord by this expression asserted his divinity and eternal existence, as the great I AM, appears evident from the use of the present tense, instead of the past tense, from its being in answer to the Jews, who enquired whether he had seen Abraham, and from its being thus understood by the multitude, who were exasperated at it to such a degree that they took up stones to stone him. The ancient Jews not only believed that the Messiah was superior to and Lord of all the patriarchs, and even of angels, but that his celestial nature existed with God from whom it emanated, before the creation, and that the creation was effected by his ministry.

The Lord Jesus Christ was Absolutely God The Great "I Am" Come to Earth In Human Form as the Long Awaited Messiah
Now how much plainer can it be that the Watchtower have erred in believing that only their rendering of the Tetragramatton is the 'name' of the Lord! The Tetragrammaton having no vowels has quite a number of ways it could be spoken in the English language as follows: Jehovah, Jihovih, Jahevih, Johavoh, Juhevoh, Juhuvuh, Jahavuh, etc., or Yohevuh, and so on and on with many many more possible names inserting vowels in the consonant letters using different vowels. So how can they be dogmatic and say they are using the true name "Jehovah' when they call themselves 'Jehovah Witnesses?' True it is, that in Exodus 6:3 the Lord Almighty told Moses that He was not known by the name Hebrew/JHVH or Jehovah or possible English language rendition of JHVH, and then in Psalm 83:18 the same rendering YHVH. The 'English' rendering of JHVH certainly cannot absolutely define the unknown correct pronunciation. The Word of God settles the question. Now we shall get back to proving the superiority of the Aramaic eastern Biblical text in proving our Savior was indeed 'God come in the form of a man, and not merely a common mortal man coming to represent God as His prophet or messenger.

Isaiah 43:10-11, & 44:8 Prove Clearly the 'word/logos' in John 1:1 was Not a Created Being!

"Ye are my witnesses saith the Lord, and my servant whom I have chosen; that ye may know and believe me, and understand that I am He; before me there was no God formed, <u>neither shall there be after me.</u> I even I am the Lord: and beside me there is no Savior." Then in 44:8. "Fear ye not, neither be afraid, have not I told thee from that time and have declared it? Ye are my witnesses. Is there a God beside me? Yea there is no God, I know not any.'

John 1:1. In the beginning was the Word and the Word was with God and the Word was God. Verse 14, "…and the Word was made flesh and dwelt among us, and we beheld His glory, the glory as of the only begotten of the Father full of grace and truth."

As well I Timothy 3:16 tells us, "…and without controversy great is the mystery of Godliness. God was manifest in the flesh, justified in the Spirit, seen of angels, preached unto the Gentiles, believed on in the world, received up into glory."

These verses bring out the following truth…

1. There is one and only one Savior, Jesus Christ the only begotten Son of God. His physical body was begotten by the overshadowing of the Spirit of God, or more correctly His body was supernaturally conceived by the Spirit of God in the womb of the virgin Mary. His physical body was thus created independently by the Father to come into the world, giving the pre-existent second person of the Trinity, the great 'I AM' the Word,,. a body in which to live in for eternity, and thus identifying Him as 'God come in the flesh.' No other being,

whether human or angelic, can be identified as an '*only begotten Son of God!*'

Truly our Lord Jesus Christ is/was God come in the flesh, as the 'only' (note the word <u>only</u>) begotten Son of God. Colossians 2:9 should well settle the question whether Jesus was indeed literally God come in the form of human flesh: "For in Him (Yeshua in Aramaic) dwelleth all the fullness of the Godhead bodily." Even a casual reading of the New Testament clearly shows Jesus to have exhibited all of the attributes of Almighty God! He had all power to raise the dead, heal the sick restore sight to the blind, read the people's minds, etc, etc. To those who falsely claim that we as Christians are 'sons of God' just as Jesus was 'a' son of God so not equal with God, we answers as follows: We as Christians are placed into the family of God by spiritual adoption and not by being 'begotten' as was Jesus our God and Savior who came to earth through the virgin birth. John 3:16, speaking of Jesus "…that God gave His **only begotten** son." Also John 1:1 "…the word was with God and the word was God" and vs. 14 "…and the Word was made flesh and dwelt among us and we beheld His glory, the glory as of the **only begotten** of the Father full of grace and truth. Ephesians 1:5, "Having predestinated us unto the adoption of children by Jesus Christ to Himself according to the good pleasure of His will."

Simply said, there was one and only one male human 'body' begotten or birthed into existence in this world by Almighty God, YHVH, and that was the physical body which the 'Word' entered into upon that bodies creation in the womb of the virgin Mary! That spiritual being called the 'Word' was clearly identified as God Himself!

2. That the <u>Word</u> and <u>God</u> are one in the same, in literal essence and Deity! Truly the 'essence of the Son' naturally is the identical essence of the Father making Jesus the only begotten Son to be equal in essence as His Father, making Jesus equal to, and the same as God! Again John 1:1 and 14.

3. That God Almighty, the great "I AM," did not create another lesser god, (as the Watchtower claim) and that verily the 'Word' was the Savior come into the World to bring salvation to all of mankind.

4. That Isaiah clearly shows there was not a 'greater God' who created a lesser 'god.' The Watchtower plainly infer such that the Almighty God, created the lesser (small 'god) by adding the unwarranted definite article 'a' before the last reference to God in Jn. 1:1. How much plainer can it be when the LORD stated, "… that ye may know and believe me, and understand that I am He; before me there was no God formed, **neither shall there be after me.**"

5. That the Greek/Aramaic originals etc., do not support the addition of the definite article 'a' before the last God in Jn.1:1, making Jesus a 'created being.' The New World Translation attacks the Deity of Christ. Interesting it is that the NWT is the only translation in 2000 years that does just that! So… that would mean until Charles Taze Russell came along (lived from 1852 to 1916) all biblical manuscripts were in error in teaching that Jesus was the same as the great I AM! It needs be remembered that the 1611 K.J.V. has always been known as the 'Trinity Bible." The oldest manuscripts in the world, including the Siniatic, Vaticanus, and Alexanderian all clearly show the Lord Jesus Christ was second person of the Trinity, 'God come in the flesh.'

Aramaic Proven to Be the Language of Jesus and Writers of the Original New Testament

Following is testimony from Rev. Glenn David Bauscher which utterly destroys the "Greek Primacy Theory," or the false notion that the New Testament was originally written in Greek. The New Testament was originally written in Aramaic, then translated to Greek as the command was to the 'Jews first (Aramaic first) and also to the Greek (next etc).

Quoting Rev. Bauscher. "The testimony of Josephus is quite clear on the point of Greek not being a language of Israel in the 1st century. Josephus was not fluent in Greek, by his own admission. He had to apply himself to learn Greek; it was obviously not the native tongue of the Jews there and there were few Jews who learned it well, as Jews were not encouraged to do so. (Please see Rev. Bauscher's web site at aramaicnt.net.)

Note: The Peshitta says, "to the Jew first, and also to the Aramaean." Act 19:10 And this continued for two years until all who dwelt in Asia heard the word of THE LORD JEHOVAH, Jews and Aramaeans.

> Act 19:17 And this became known to all the Jews and Aramaeans dwelling in Ephesaus and great fear fell upon all of them, and the name of Our Lord Yeshua The Messiah was exalted.
>
> Act 20:21 While I was testifying to the Jews and to the Aramaeans about returning home to the presence of God and the faith in Our Lord Yeshua The Messiah.
>
> Act 21:28 As they appealed and they were saying, "Men, sons of Israel, help! This is the man who opposes our people, teaching in every place against the law and against this place, and he also has brought an Aramaean into The Temple and has defiled this holy place." *

Rom 1:16 For I am not ashamed of The Gospel, because it is the power of God for the life of all who believe in it, whether of The Judeans first, or of the Aramaeans*.

Rom 2:9 Suffering and trouble, to every person who cultivates wickedness, to the Jews first and to the Aramaeans*,

Rom 2:10 But glory, honor and peace to everyone who cultivates good, to the Jews first, and to the Aramaeans.

Rom 3:9 What, then? Are we held to be greater because we have precedence? We have determined about the Jews and about the Aramaeans that they are all under sin, *

Rom 10:12 And he makes no distinction in this, not for the Jews, neither for the Aramaeans, for he is The One LORD JEHOVAH to all of them, who is rich with everyone who calls to him.

1Co 1:22 Because the Jews ask for signs and the Aramaeans* seek philosophy.

1Co 1:23 But we preach The Messiah as crucified, a scandal to the Judeans and madness to the Aramaeans*.

1Co 1:24 But to those who are called, Jews and Aramaeans, The Messiah is the power of God and the wisdom of God.

1Co 10:32 Be without violation to the Jews and to the Aramaeans* and to the Church of God,

1Co 12:13 For we also are baptized by The One Spirit into one body, whether Jews or Aramaeans or Servants or free men, and we are all made to drink The One Spirit.

Gal 2:3 Even Titus, an Aramaean* who was with me, was not compelled to be circumcised.

Gal 3:28 There is neither Jew nor Aramaean*, neither Servant nor Free person, neither male nor female, for all of you are one in Yeshua The Messiah.

Col 3:11 Where there is neither Jew nor Aramaean, neither circumcision nor uncircumcision, neither Greeks nor Barbarians, neither Servant nor Freeman, but The Messiah is all and in every person*.

An Aramaean was an Aramaic speaking Gentile. Greeks are not mentioned in this context. Aramaic was the lingua franca (universal language) of the Middle East and Asia. Greek translation came later for the Greek speaking Romans.

Quoting: Historian Josephus,

"I have taken great pains to obtain the Greek learning and understand the elements of the Greek language" How does this come to mean that "Greek was a primary or second language in Israel"? "Our nation does not encourage those that learn the language of many nations"- Josephus. "I have so accustomed myself to speak our own language, that I cannot pronounce Greek with sufficient exactness?"

How can anyone believe that Greek was a primary or second language in Israel? How can such an idea be supported in face of such testimony of such a 1st century Israeli scholar, Priest and historian of Israel? Notice also that Josephus speaks of only one language - "our own language"; there was only one common language (Aramaic) and no mention of "languages".

Elsewhere Josephus wrote:

"I have proposed to myself, for the sake of such as live under the government of the Romans, to translate those books into the Greek tongue, which I formerly composed in the

language of our country, and sent to the Upper Barbarians"
End of quote.

Whiston's note on the "upper Barbarians": Who these Upper Barbarians, remote from the sea, were, Josephus himself will inform us, sect. 2, viz. "… the Parthians and Babylonians, and remotest Arabians [of the Jews among them]; besides the Jews beyond Euphrates, and the Adiabeni, or Assyrians. Whence we also learn that these Parthians, Babylonians, the remotest Arabians, [or at least the Jews among them,] as also the Jews beyond Euphrates, and the Adiabeni, or Assyrians, understood Josephus's Hebrew, or rather Chaldaic, books of The Jewish War, before they were put into the Greek language.(Chaldaic is Aramaic)

The Preface to Josephus' Antiquities has the following: 2. "Now I have undertaken the present work, as thinking it will appear to all the Greeks worthy of their study; for it will contain all our antiquities, and the constitution of our government, as interpreted out of the Hebrew Scriptures…I grew weary and went on slowly, it being a large subject, and a difficult thing to translate our history into a foreign, and to us unaccustomed language…"

There were some Hellenists in Israel, but that very term demolishes the idea that all or most 1st century Jews in Israel spoke Greek. A Hellenist is by definition, "a Greek speaking Jew". If the common Christian view of 1st century language of Israel were correct, then all Jews in Israel were Hellenists! But the NT mentions the Hellenists as a separate group in Israel. Ac 6:1 And in those days, when the number of the disciples was multiplied, there arose a murmuring of the Grecians against the Hebrews, because their widows were neglected in the daily ministration. Acts 9:29 And he spake boldly in the name of the Lord Jesus, and disputed against the Grecians: but they went about to slay him. Ac 11:20 And some of them were men of Cyprus and Cyrene, which, when they were come to Antioch, spake unto the Grecians (1675), preaching the Lord Jesus. "

The Eastern Aramaic Peshitta Alone Containing the Hebrew Translated Tetragrammaton (As Aramaic 'yah') Clearly Identifies the Lord Jesus Christ As God Come In the Flesh!

One very false teaching of the Watchtower, is that early scribes at some point decided to remove the Tetragrammaton from the first century Greek manuscripts (clearly false). Since the original New Testament was first written in Aramaic, the language of Jesus and His disciples, and that it did indeed contain the Tetragrammaton, *(translated as 'Yah' it's equal in Aramaic)* makes them only half right. In translating the originals from Aramaic into Greek, unfortunately there was no equivalent Greek term for the Tetragrammaton 'Yah' so it was dropped, and the Greek 'Kurios' or 'Theos' was used for 'Lord' and 'God'. Clearly they are wrong in thinking that the originals were in Greek containing the actual Tetragrammaton. Luke Wayne, contributor to carm.org 10/11/16 states the following:

"All manuscripts and ancient translations use the word Lord and do not use YHWH. This only makes sense if Lord is the original form. Further, when Jews of that day wrote letters or books, they avoided YHWH and instead used God, Master, or Lord. Some Jews and all the Earliest Christians were clearly using copies of the Septuagint that used the word "Lord" in place of the divine name. This is the culture in which the New Testament was written. When Paul wrote his letters as a first century Jew, all the evidence points to the idea that he would not use the name YHWH. When Luke quoted from the Greek Septuagint, the evidence shows us he was probably quoting from a copy that already used the word "Lord." All of this reinforces what we see in every single New Testament manuscript and in every single early quotation of the New Testament in early writings: That the New Testament was written using the word "Lord" in place of the divine name YHVH or JHVH. The New Testament never contained the word YHWH, and so our translations of the New Testament today should not contain the word "Jehovah." End quote.

Of course (as the last statement shows) Mr. Wayne also is under the mistaken idea that the New Testament was originally written in Greek, rather than in Aramaic, as most scholars and theological schools today believe. He no doubt is correct that copies or translations of the originals into the Greek etc. did not contain the Tetragrammaton YHWH. Yes, very sad it is that in translation from the original Pehsitta Aramaic into Greek, and then into English, has somewhat weakened the clear teaching that Jesus Christ was clearly God/YHVH/YAH come in the flesh. We shall get to that next. It is well to repeat a simple fact, which any honest Christian can see for himself, that being that the Rev. Glenn David Bauscher (perhaps now the greatest most honorable scholar in all of church history) has irrefutably proven the original autographed New Testament penned under Divine inspiration by the pen of the Apostles, was:

1. Written in Aramaic

2. That such can be proven by the underlying divine codes contained in the text, and can be mathematically and scientifically proven down to the last letter as being word for word and letter for letter, identically the same as the autographs. Go to aramaicnt.com to obtain the original (now restored) Peshitta Aramaic interlinear Bible, and his book on Bible codes. His findings indeed are truly a miracle, preserved to be discovered in these last days of computer science! No atheist or disbeliever now, can deny the verbal inspiration of the Bible! It is proven by the mathematical bible codes, and of course by the fulfilled prophecies.

3. Rev. Bauscher has irrefutably shown that the divine codes contained in the Aramaic Peshitta disappear, when just one letter or word is added or taken away. This makes the Aramaic Peshitta he has restored without error and 100% equal to the

original autographs! Our Lord promised that though heaven and earth pass away, His word would endure i.e. be preserved forever! The biblical fact that 'all scripture is given by inspiration of God, necessitates the preservation of God's word through a verifiable, concrete scientific means. Rev. Bauscher has discovered that means, and truly his name should be revered and honored in church history!

Getting back to the Watchtower: In their zeal to promote the Tetragrammaton (due to their interest in keeping their name 'Jehovah –JHVH-Witnesses,') interesting it is that the Tetragrammaton translated as Aamaic'YAH' is found only the Aramaic N.T. Peshitta, and actually contradicts their denial of the deity of Christ. (Of course the Tetragrammaton is well known in the Hebrew Old Testament scriptures.) Fact is though; it irrefutably proves His deity.

Chapter Six

DO JEHOVAH'S WITNESSES BELIEVE IN JESUS?

Watchtower proponents aggressively deny His deity as follows: "Yes. We believe in Jesus, who said: "I am the way and the truth and the life. No one comes to the Father except through me." (John 14:6) We have faith that Jesus came to earth from heaven and gave his perfect human life as a ransom sacrifice. (Matthew 20:28) His death and resurrection make it possible for those exercising faith in him to gain everlasting life. (John 3:16) We also believe that Jesus is now ruling as King of God's heavenly Kingdom, which will soon bring peace to the entire earth. (Revelation 11:15) However, we take Jesus at his word when he said: "The Father is greater than I am." (John 14:28) So we do not worship Jesus, as we do not believe that he is Almighty God". (Quotation from 'JW.ORG.')

Watchtower Corruption of John 10:30-33
New World Watchtower translation. (jw.org). 30 I and the Father are one." Once again the Jews picked up stones to stone him.32 Jesus replied to them: "I displayed to you many fine works from the Father. For which of those works are you stoning me?"33 The Jews answered him: "We are stoning you, not for a fine work, but for blasphemy for you, although being a man, make yourself a god."

K.J.V. **I and my Father are one.** Then the Jews took up stones again to stone Him. Jesus answered, Many good works have I shewed you from my father for which of those works do ye stone me? The Jews answered Him saying, For a good work we stone thee not, but for blasphemy and because that **thou being a man, makest thyself God.**

The Peshitta original restored interlinear New Testament in Aramaic/English. (Restored by Rev. David Glenn Bauscher). Vs 30. "I and my Father, We are One." 31. And the Judeans picked up stones again to stone him. 32. And Yeshua said to them, "Many excellent works from the presence of my Father I have shown you. For which of those works are you stoning me?" 33. The Judeans were saying to him, "It is not for excellent works that we are stoning you, but because you blaspheme, and as you are a man, you make yourself God."

Reasons the Watchtower 'Jesus Was *A God*' Will Not Stand!

1. Our Lord plainly said in the inspired text, "I and the Father are one." He did not say "I and the Father are one in our purpose." His statement must be taken as He said that He and the Father are one. I.e. they are one and the same literally God in the flesh.

2. The reason our Lord could not have meant '...I and the Father are one in purpose' is that the immediate response of the Jews to the 'I and the Father are one' statement, was they wanted to stone Him. That proves they understood that Jesus was fully equating Himself with Almighty God to which they regarded as blasphemy. Blasphemy under Jewish law was plainly a sin worthy of death (Lev.24:13-16). They were ready to stone Jesus to death for equating Himself with God, not for supposedly (Watchtower perverted translation) claiming to be 'a god' or a lesser god than Almighty God. The fact is there was no death penalty for someone claiming to be 'a

god.' The Romans had many 'gods' and even some Roman Emperors claimed that they were 'a god.' This is another perversion of God's precious word concerning our Lord Jesus supposedly being 'a god.' See the Watchtower poor translation of John 1:1, where they dishonestly translated that Jesus was "the Word who was a god."

3. So we are to believe that for about 2000 years of church history the thousands and thousands of Biblical manuscript in existence were in error and not faithful to translation until the New World Translation (Watchtower Bible) in the 20th century?

4. Then the following scriptures which are from the Watchtower Bible contradicts their own 'interpretation of John 10, because they were forced to translate them correctly!

5. This also clearly proves their translation of John 1:1 should not have been translated as '…and the Word was with God and the Word was a god.'

Watchtower N.W.T. of John 20:27-28

Next he (Jesus) said to Thomas: "Put your finger here, and see my hands, and take your hand and stick it into my side, and stop doubting but believe."

In answer Thomas said to him: "My Lord and my God!" (*Clearly Thomas was looking at Jesus as his Lord and his God! Editor*).

Watchtower N.W.T. of 1 John 5:20 Following

But we know that the Son of God has come and he has given us insight, so that we may gain the knowledge of the one who is true. And we are in union with the one who is true, by means of his Son Jesus Christ. This is the true God and life everlasting. ('God' here is Alaha/Aramaic Elohim or God Almighty) and life everlasting. (Also the Watchtower knew they could not get by with translating this verse as…"This is the true god and…"). The below verse makes this so plain. From the Textus Receptus which includes over 2000 manuscripts, and first and foremost from the original Peshitta Aramaic. Also add the Siniatic, Vaticanus, Alexandrian which date from 301-450 A.D.

1 John 5:20

And we know that the Son of Alaha (Aramaic Elohim or God) is come and hath given us an understanding that we may know Him that is true and we are in Him that is true even in His Son Yeshua Meshikha. This is the true Alaha and Eternal Life.

Important Biblical Definitions

For a full understanding of this problem, it is a must to compare Biblical terms in the Aramaic Peshitta to translations in the Greek, English etc.

1. **'Mar'**: Meaning 'Master or Lord' in the Aramaic

2. **'Mari'**: Also Aramaic meaning '…my LORD.'

3. **'Adon'**: Hebrew meaning 'LORD.'

4. **'Adoni'**: Meaning 'My LORD.'

5. **'YHVH or JHVH:** the very sacred Tetragrammaton not a *'name'* meant to be spoken by the Hebrews ('Yes true there are transliterations such as Yehwah' or 'Jehovah' but strictly speculative. Actually the Watchtower has no scriptural right to use it as their name!) This unspoken Hebrew reference to God is used thorough out the Tanakh (Old Testament) over 6500 times. This is the eternal, memorial reference to Almighty God. Yah- the short version of YHVH (Yahweh)

used in "hallelu-Yah (praise Yah), king Hezekiah (KhizqiYah Yah has strengthened), etc.

6. **'Yah'**: The Aramaic short/or equal for the Tetragrammaton YHVH namely the God of Israel!

7. **'MarYah'**: Contraction of 'Mar' and 'Yah' or 'Master/Lord Yah.'

8. **'Alaha' also transliterated 'Eloah'**: Aramaic equivalent of the Hebrew 'Elohim' (the God of Israel).

9. **'Yeshua'**: Yehoshua/Yeshua is the Hebrew name for Jesus. It means "Yahweh [**the Lord**] **is Salvation**." The English spelling of Yeshua is "Joshua." However, when translated from Hebrew into Greek, (in which the New Testament was written), **Iesous is** the Greek transliteration of the Hebrew name, and its English spelling **is** "Jesus.

Several points come to mind here, which the Watchtower has plainly overlooked. The first is the firmly Biblical established fact that the Lord Jesus Christ is clearly identified in the New (and of course Old) Testament as being the one who was responsible for creating all things that exists, whether it be in the physical or spiritual realm! Consider the following translated directly from the original Aramaic Peshitta,, the original first original Bible given by the Spirit of God:

1 Corinthians 12:3

Wherefore I give you to understand that no man speaking by the Spirit of Alaha calleth Yeshua accursed and that no man can say that Yeshua is MarYah (Lord/God) but by the Holy Spirit.

1 John 5:20

And we know that the Son of Alaha (Aramaic Elohim or God is come and hath given us an understanding that we may know Him that is true and we are in Him that is true even in His Son Yeshua Meshikha. This is the true Alaha and Eternal Life.

Colossians 1:13-16

...and hath translated un into the kingdom of His beloved Son: In whom we have redemption through His blood, even the forgiveness of sins: Who is the image of the invisible God, the first born of every creature: for by Him (i.e.-Yeshua/Jesus God creator) were all things created that are in heaven and that are upon earth, visible and invisible whether thrones of dominions, or principalities, or powers, all things were created by Him and for Him. (Now notice just who in the Old Testament is identified by the Tetragrammaton as the all powerful Creator! Notice as follows, 'LORD'= YHVH):

Psalm 134:2-3

Lift up your hands in the sanctuary and bless the Lord, the Lord that made heaven and earth bless thee out of Zion.

Psalm 124:8

Our help is in the name of the Lord, who made heaven and earth....

Genesis 1:1

In the beginning God created the heavens and the earth...

Hebrews 1:8-9/Psalm 45:6-7

But unto the Son He saith, Thy throne O Alaha, is forever and ever a scepter of righteousness is the scepter of thy kingdom. Thou hast loved righteousness and hated iniquity, there Alaha, even thy Alaha hath anointed thee with the oil of gladness above thy fellows. And Thou MarYah (Lord/YHVH) in the beginning hast laid the foundation of the earth and the heavens are the works of thine hands.

Now you and I are not the image of the invisible God, since we can never be equal with Almighty God, but Yeshua/Jesus the Christ certainly is, especially since He by incarnation is the exact image of Elohim, and since He as Yeshua is 'THE SON OF GOD.' Yeshua is the only one in the Word of God identified as "THE ONLY BEGOTTEN SON OF GOD." Simple fact is, one member of the Trinity, condescended into this sinful world, and entered the embryo created by and for Him in the womb of the Virgin Mary, and was born Jesus of Nazareth, Savior of the world. John 1:1 and 14 make this irrefutably clear. "In the beginning was the Word and the Word was with God and the Word was God... All things were made by Him and without Him was not anything made that was made...And the Word was made flesh and dwelt among us, and we beheld His glory as of the only begotten of the Father full of grace and truth.

The Watchtower translation of John 1:1 is plainly skewed as follows: (JW.ORG New World Translation)… "In the beginning was the Word and the Word was with God and the Word was <u>a god</u>." The following facts need to be brought out exposing this gross error in translation.

1. Absolutely not one Peshitta Aramaic, Greek, Latin, manuscript from the first few centuries, or of subsequent centuries (which were copies of the original autographs, or copies of copies of the originals etc.) states that the "Word" was '**a god**'. That of course makes the 'Word' a lesser god created by Elohim. In fact the scriptures plainly state that Almighty God, clearly identified by the Tetragrammaton in the Old Testament as the LORD, not only was the creator of all things, but that HE clearly states that he never created a 'lesser god or

Savior!.' …" Notice Isaiah 43:10-11. "You are my witnesses, saith YHVH (Yahweh, MarYah in Aramaic) and my servant whom I have chosen in order that you may know and believe Me, and understand that I am He. Before Me there was no God formed, and there will be none after Me. I am I am YHVH (Yahweh, MarYah in Aramaic) and besides me there is no Savior." Isaiah 43:14 "…thus saith YHVH (*Yahweh MarYah in Aramaic*) Your Holy One, the Creator of Israel, your King."

2. Next notice that the 'Word' in the above verses in John, is clearly identified as the all powerful Creator who created all things! This goes hand in hand with Col. 1:13-16 which irrefutably states that the Lord Jesus Christ was the Creator of all things.

3. How clear it is from Isaiah that there is one and only one Savior in the universe, and that one is YHWH who was manifested in the flesh as the 'WORD' which became flesh, the Savior of the world.

Notice the following scriptures which clearly and unmistakably identify the Lord God of Israel and the Savior of the world as being one in the same.

Psalm 146:6

Happy is he that hath the God of Jacob for his help, whose hope is in the Lord his God who made heaven and earth, the sea and all that is in them who keepeth truth forever.

Now clearly there are two identified in John 1:1, first God the Almighty, and then secondly the 'Word.' The Watchtower attempt to say that the 'Word' (supposedly a created inferior 'god') was *given* power to create all things in heaven and earth, when in fact no scripture supports such doctrine! As we just pointed out, all ancient Holy Scripture manuscripts state clearly and unequivocally that the 'Word' and 'God' are equally one in the same. That there is no definite article 'a' before 'god, but was added to the verse by the Watchtower proves the 'Word was God!' Watchtower rejection of the doctrine of the Triune God Head (one God in three persons) forces them to this false conclusion. Remember the Hebrew plural term "Elohim" in Genesis 1:1 (i.e. 'In the beginning God or Elohim, created the heavens and earth,) is further clarified by verse 26 where God said, "Let *us* make man in *our* image."

Berry's Interlinear Greek English New Testament gives the exact Greek text and its English equivalent as follows... "In the beginning was the Word, and the Word was with God and God was the Word." Thomas in John 20:28 clearly identified Jesus as his Lord and God when he be held Him in His resurrected body, seeing the nail prints in His hands and wound in His side by proclaiming "My Lord and my God." Many other verses back this up like 1 Jn. 5:20, "…even in his Son Jesus Christ, this is the true God and eternal life." An amazing fact concerning this verse comes to light in the Watchtower (perverted) translation of the New Testament! Looking to the Watchtower mis-translation of this verse (JW.ORG New World Translation) it is clearly seen that they were forced to translate this verse correctly, and thus contradict their skewed translation of John 1:1. As follows quoting verbatim: "And we are in union with the one who is true, by means of ***His Son Jesus Christ. This is the true God*** and life everlasting."

Note: The following declare Jesus is The Life: 1 Jn 1:1-3; 1Jn 5:12, 1Jn 5:20, 1Jn 1:1-3, 1Jn 4:9; Joh 1:4, Joh 5:21, Joh 5:26, Joh 11:25-26, Joh 14:6; Col 3:3-4; Rev 22:1. As He is the Life, so is He also The Only True God, as 1 John 5:20 declares: "this is the true God and eternal life." The One who is "the only True God" is also eternal life! Yeshua is His name!

Yeshua was truly God come in the flesh. 1 Tim. 3:16, "And without controversy great is the mystery of godliness, God was manifest in the flesh…" So… the Watchtower needs to carefully read Isaiah 43:10 to understand once and for all, that the Almighty God did not create a lesser 'god' who supposedly became Savior of the world. For Almighty God to have created a lesser 'god' and then give him the same powers He has to create all in heavens and earth would make that lesser 'god' equal (?) with Himself. Only an omnipotent all powerful God could have created all there is in heaven and in earth! Fact is there is only one God, manifested in three persons as Genesis Chapter 18 so clearly shows. (See this author's book available on Amazon etc, "Abraham the Trinity and Lot Exonerated Genesis 18 & 19.")

John 1:1

The oldest complete perfect originally preserved manuscript in the world; the Aramaic Peshitta proves…

The word was God and the Lord Jesus Christ was that word!

Rev. Glenn David Bauscher perhaps the most famous Biblical scholar in all of church history has discovered the original letter perfect original New Testament from the first and second century, predating all other manuscripts, including the original Greek text. Rev. Bauscher has discovered divine codes or hidden 'watermarks' if you will, in the Aramaic N.T. which absolutely verifies scientifically and mathematically, that the manuscript he has discovered is identical to the original autographed Biblical manuscripts. Taking away one letter or word, or adding one letter or word and the codes disappear. (Go to his web site to obtain this Bible and books to explain the coded text.) Quoting from this original Divine text as follows: "In the Origin… existing…had been…the Word…and that…Word…existing…had been…with…God…and God…Himself…was…that…Word.

Now enter Charles Taze Russell born 1852 (died 1916 age 64) some one thousand nine hundred years after the Aramaic Peshitta was penned. Russell absolutely denied the Deity of Christ, and was the one who established what became later know as the Jehovah Witnesses. He of course is directly responsible for the so called 'New World Translation of the scriptures which repudiates the Deity of our Savior. According to him evidently the gates of hell prevailed against the church for those thousands of years, until he came into this world with his false theology! (The Mormons, Jews, Muslims and others who deny the deity of Christ would be well to take note of Rev. Bauscher's works.) Truth will stand examination.

Notice again the New World Translation amazingly was correctly translated in another verse to contradict their perversion of John 1:1.

Watchtower N.W.T. of John 20:27-28
*Next he (Jesus) **said to Thomas: "Put your finger here, and see my hands, and take your hand and stick it into my side, and stop doubting* but believe."** [28] in answer Thomas said to him: **"My Lord and my God!"***

The Watchtower have made a claim concerning their belief that in the first century A.D. one or more Greek manscripts had the Tetragrammaton in its text.

It is only fair at this point for this author, to give special recognition to Roy A. Reinhold at codes04@charter.net for the following study, proving that the Aramaic Peshitta and the Tetragramaton therein, prove irrefutably that Jesus Christ is/was literally (JHVH) God come in the flesh! Thank you and God bless your studies brother Reinhold. This writer/author (myself) has been amazed that such a monumental revelation as this, has been hidden/obscured for centuries and centuries due to unclear and vastly weakened Bible translations of the Aramaic Peshitta into other tongues and languages. I am sure someone will be asking, "What is the huge difference whether someone believes that the Lord Jesus Christ is or was God come in the flesh or not?" To which we answer: Because a person cannot find Biblical salvation and pardon from sin in this life (if they deny the deity of Christ!) Upon death without the new birth, a person will be consigned to Hell and then later to the Lake of Fire to be punished according to their sins. Simply put, no one can become saved or born again if they reject the deity of Jesus!

Reason being, if Jesus was only a fallible man, or a created being then He would be disqualified from being our sin offering on the cross of Calvary (as God/man) before Almighty God. Only Jesus, being the perfect spotless, sinless Lamb of God could atone for our sins. Not only that, but the scriptures in the Old Testament (and new) clearly taught that the Messiah would be "God come in the flesh" and the scriptures cannot be broken (they must literally be fulfilled to the smallest jot and title), Anyone rejecting the deity of Jesus, upon death, he, or she will be consigned to Hell and then later to the Lake of Fire to be punished according to their sins. Simply put, no one can become saved or born again if they reject the deity of Jesus! Heaven or Hell, forgiveness of sins hangs in the balance. (*Proceeding now with Reinholds studies, which will be somewhat condensed from his originals*).

Chapter Seven

THE PESHITTA AND THE DIVINITY OF CHRIST JESUS YESHUA

Use of the Name of God (YHVH/JHVH) in the New Testament and the Divinity of Jesus (Yeshua)

When something is translated from one language to another, there is always somewhat of a step down in conveying what is written from one language to another. There is always something lost, or some truth slightly modified to some degree. That is the same with the manuscripts which were translated from the original autographs, and then naturally from copies of the originals into other languages, and so on. While the A.V. is a beautiful translation, it is none the less a translation subject to the same weaknesses of any translation to some degree no matter how small that may be. None the less all of the fundamental doctrines of the faith remain intact and in that sense perfectly revealed. *(The A.V. K.J.V 1611 version has been named by some as the 'Trinity Bible.')*

Mr. Reinhold scanned the entire Aramaic N.T. Peshitta for every scripture where Y.H.V.H was given in Aramaic as 'Yah' (clearly the name of Almighty God), and is used for Yeshua (Jesus). He found some 30 verses where this was the case! Clearly so we might add! Again, only in the ancient Eastern Aramaic Peshitta does this occur. On the other hand, the Greek N.T. manuscripts use the name 'Kurios' (LORD) or 'Theos' (God) in the exact same place where the divine name (YHVH or 'Yah') is used in the Aramaic! True it is that many English translations use the name "LORD or Lord" for the divine name YHVH as found in the Tanakh Hebrew Old Testament. This is proof positive that the Greek translations came from the Peshitta and not vice versa as so many have been taught in colleges and seminaries for hundreds and hundreds of years. History of the Eastern Aramaic Church clearly shows that they obtained their copies of the original manuscripts directly from those of the hands of the apostles. They needed not translations since they spoke the same language of the apostles and disciples.

Emperor Constantine and the Council of Nicea
"Constantine the Great, was a Roman emperor from 306 to 337. Constantine served with distinction under emperors Diocletian and Galerius campaigning in the eastern provinces against barbarians and the Persians, before being recalled west in 305 to fight under his father in Britain. After his father's death in 306, Constantine was acclaimed as emperor by the army at Eboracum (York). He emerged victorious in the civil wars against emperors Maxentius and to become sole ruler of the Roman Empire by 324." (From Wikipedia and following (One can only imagine Constantines' service to Diocletian (who so hated Christians) that before his conversion to Christianity the terrors he must have brought them.)

"The First Council of Nicaea, the first general council in the history of the Church, was convened by the Roman emperor Constantine the Great upon the recommendations of a synod led by the bishop Hosius of Corduba in the Eastertide of 325, or rather convened by Hosius and supported by Constantine. This synod had been charged with investigation of the trouble brought about by the Arian controversy in the Greek-speaking east. To most bishops, the teachings of Arius were heretical and dangerous to the salvation of souls. In the summer of 325, the bishops of all provinces were summoned to Nicaea, a place reasonably accessible to many delegates, particularly those of Asia Minor, Georgia, Armenia, Syria, Egypt, Greece, and Thrace."

According to Warren H. Carroll, in the Council of Nicaea, "The Church had taken her first great step to define revealed doctrine more precisely in response to a challenge from a heretical theology."

The fact that the Church of the East, was not in favor with Constantine (nor under his control) and not invited to the council of Nicea in 325 A.D. thankfully prevented corruption of the eastern Aramaic bible, as was not the case with the Syriac Bible. The clear evidence is that the N.T. books were authored in Aramaic with Hebrew/Aramaic block letters books, and later translated into Greek, corroborating the Church of the East history. (Interesting is that Mel Gibson's Roman Catholic advisors, led him to do his film 'Passion of the Christ' in Aramaic to be more true to history). During the first few hundred years, great division broke out in professing Christendom between Arius, (who taught that Jesus was not of the same substance as God [YHVH] but was a created being, perhaps even that Jesus was the same as Michael the arch angel), and Constantine who legalized Christianity in 313 A.D. Constantine determined that a church wide council need be called to debate and come to firm conclusions concerning the true nature of Christ. Thus hoping to settle these differences he called for the council in 325 A.D.

So, the main purpose of the Council (following from Wikipedia) "…was to resolve disagreements arising from within the Church of Alexandria over the nature of the Son in his relationship to the Father: in particular, whether the Son had been 'begotten' by the Father from his own being, and therefore having no beginning, or else created out of nothing, and therefore having a beginning. This synod had been charged with investigation of the trouble brought about by the Arian controversy in the Greek-speaking east. The outcome of the council follows: St. Alexander of Alexandria and Athanasius took the first position; the popular presbyter Arius, from whom the term Arianism comes, took the second. The Council decided against the Arians overwhelmingly (of the estimated 250–318 attendees, all but two agreed to sign the creed and these two, along with Arius, were banished to Illyria."

Constantine exiled those who came but would not sign the Nicean Creed and ordered Arius's books burned. The Arians believed that Jesus' nature was (Greek term) 'homoiousios' (like but not same substance), while the Nicean term was 'homoousios' (of the same substance) to say Yeshua Jesus, was equal to, and the same as God. Unitarians and Watchtower have very similar beliefs that Jesus was not literally God come in the flesh, but a created (later highly exalted) being. (Some semi-Arians believe Jesus was later exalted to become equal with God). It needs to be added here that during this period there was a religious group called the Ebionites who denied both the Deity and the virgin birth of our Savior. These views are very similar to Arianism. Then the Watchtower society holds similar views of Yeshua, namely that He had a pre-human existence as the 'Logos' that He was not Deity but is the "Logos" (or a 'force' from the Father) the Word of God).

Constantine therefore (having ordered Arius' books to be destroyed because Arius taught Yeshua was not equal with YHWH but rather was a created being who later was exalted to somehow become God), exiled those who rejected Biblical doctrine of "Yeshua's equality of substance with God." The Arians did not believe that Yeshua was co-eternal, co-existent, and co-equal (also pre-existent with) the Father God, but that Yeshua was created like the angels.

One may ask just what is the importance of the Word of God being studied in the original Aramaic/English interlinear, the language of our Savior and His disciples. The answer is simple. The Aramaic Eastern Peshitta Bible so perfectly shows the deity of Christ that when it was translated into Greek etc., that truth was somewhat compromised, due to language differences, and that of course gave rise to doctrinal error. It is no wonder that the Watchtower, (erroneously known as "Jehovah Witnesses") and others such as Unitarians and Muslims, have misunderstood the doctrine of the full Deity of Christ our LORD. Muslims hold that while Jesus was a good and great prophet (generally called Isa), none the less was not divine or the Son of God. The Koran states:

Sura An-Nisa 4-171 Koran
"O people of the Book! Commit no excesses in your religion: Nor say of God aught but the truth. Jesus Christ, the son of Mary, was (no more than) a messenger of God, and His word, which He bestowed on Mary, and a spirit proceeding from Him: so believe in God and His messengers. Say not "Trinity" desist: it will be better for you: for God is one God: Glory be to Him: (far exalted is he) above having a son. To Him belong all things in the heavens and on earth. And enough is God as Disposer of affairs."

As for the false teaching that "Allah" is the same as the Christian God "YHVH" such teaching is absolutely false. YHVH exists as a triune God head, i.e. one God in three persons, and each manifested in three separate persons.

It is immeasurably important to see just why such theological division has arisen over the Biblical doctrine of the Deity of our Savior in the first several centuries. When one examines the original Eastern Aramaic Peshitta, and then follows the translation of the same on into the Greek language, (then into English etc.), the fact can be seen that in translation, some clarity concerning the Deity of Christ is somewhat compromised or lost! No doubt the Watchtower Society has stumbled because of this obscurity and states the following: "However, we take Jesus at his word when he said: "The Father is greater than I am." (John 14:28) So we do not worship Jesus, as we do not believe that he is Almighty God". (Quotation from 'JW. ORG.') Certainly this shows the Watchtower Society has overlooked the truth that our Savior had two distinct natures which can clearly be demonstrated by scripture. He had the full nature of man, and as well had the full nature of God within the same body. He was God/Man or God fully come in human form. It is well to add here that 'man' Yeshua (Jesus) of Nazareth while virgin born, still had a fully human nature, capable of learning and developing mentally as any other normal human, who as well was tempted in all points as we are, yet without sin.

II Corinthians 5:19

> To wit, that God was in Christ, reconciling the world unto Himself, not imputing their trespasses unto them; and hath committed unto us the word of reconciliation.

Phillipians 2:6-11

> (*Yeshua/Jesus*) Who, being in the form of God, ***thought it not robbery to be equal with God:***[7] But made himself of no reputation, and took upon him the form of a servant, and was made in the likeness of men:[8] And being found in fashion as a man, he humbled himself, and became obedient unto death, even the death of the cross.[9] Wherefore God also hath highly exalted him, and given him a name which is above every name:[10] That at the name of Jesus every knee should bow, of things in heaven, and things in earth, and things under the earth;[11] And that every tongue should confess that Jesus Christ is LORD, to the glory of God the Father.

John 1:1-3 and 14

In the beginning was the Word, and the Word was with God and the Word was God. The same was in the beginning with God. All things were made by Him and without Him was not anything made that was made. Vs. 14. And the Word was made flesh and dwelt among us, and we beheld His glory as of the only begotten Son of God full of grace and truth.

Thus we can clearly see that the two natures in Yeshua were the nature of God Almighty and the physical nature of man or Yeshua conceived by the Holy Spirit and born to the virgin Mary. He was fully God/Man! As we go on we will see irrefutable facts from the Aramaic Peshitta original Bible manuscripts that Jesus Christ was literally God come in the flesh!

The original Hebrew O.T. Scripture uses the Tetragrammaton YHVH in over 6500 times to identify the God of Israel. Then when the Aramaic translation of the Old Testament came between 50 B.C. and 50 A.D. the Aramaic term 'Mar' (Lord/Master also translated into the Greek as 'Kurios.') and 'Yah' the Aramaic short for the Tetragrammaton YHVH put together was 'MarYah.' Simply put 'LORD God!' What this does is to elevate the word 'Lord' in this verse to 'LORD GOD, or 'Mar-Yah' (YHVH) in the original. This verse in the original text simply says "…And that every tongue should confess that Jesus Christ is LORD GOD to the glory of the father."

Thus the <u>Greek</u> translation of this verse and on into the English etc, can give the false impression for those who deny the Deity of our Savior that, "Yes…Jesus was Lord, as in like the king or lord of a province, but not LORD GOD. The fact is that the Greek manuscripts translated from the original Aramaic by hands of the Apostles (and immediately given to the world), had no word equal to the Tetragrammaton (or Yah Aramaic for YHVH)) and so used the Greek "Kurios (Lord/Master) and Theos (God). In this study we will shortly see many other N.T. places that 'Mar-Yah' was used in direct reference to Yeshua proving He was indeed Almighty God come in the flesh. Please remember that only, ONLY in the Aramaic Peshitta manuscripts that 'Mar-Yah' is used to identify Yeshua as, "The LORD

GOD JESUS!" It is well to add that while the Greek translations were not as clear in some instances concerning the Deity of our Lord, they all still, without question, clearly defined it in many many scriptures throughout the N.T.

Why were the scriptures translated from Hebrew into Aramaic? Answer is that the Jews went into Babylonian captivity about 597 BCE when King Nebuchadnezzar attacked Jerusalem and destroyed it. For seventy years they were in bondage until Cyrus overthrew Babylon in about 539 BCE. The lingua franca of Babylon (language of the common people and merchants) /was Aramaic which of course became the language the Jews adopted. Such being the case so Aramaic was the common language of the Jew up until and including the time of Jesus and his apostles. We have already shown that the Jewish rabbis detested the language of the Greeks, and taught it would be better to eat the flesh of swine than to speak Greek. We learned this from Jewish historian Josephus. King Cyrus in 539 BCE gave the Jews permission to return to Jerusalem to rebuild the temple. Thus due to the many years in Babylonian captivity, Aramaic the language of Babylon gave the Jews their new language.

Chapter Eight

THE ENGLISH MASTERED IN THE ORIGINAL PESHITTA

New Testament Aramaic Biblical Terms Proving the Deity of Our Savior

Were it not for the vast disagreement over just who Jesus was by so many different religious groups etc., and the fact that some translations of the originals can somewhat obscure a clear doctrine on the origin of our Savior, there would be no need for this discussions. Wonderful it is that our Lord foresaw such division and made it crystal clear about the true nature and being of our Savior. In examining the Eastern Aramaic Peshitta New Testament, all controversy is silenced, since the Peshitta irrefutably proves that the Lord Jesus was none other than YHWH come in the flesh. First though we must become acquainted with some key Aramaic words. Again it must be emphasized that we are not going to the coine' Greek manuscripts/ the Textus Receptus, the Alexanderian, Siniatic, or Vaticanus to examine this wonderful truth, but rather the Eastern Aramaic Peshitta New Testament in its original form. Following are key Aramaic words which give us the facts surroundings the Peshitta validating that Jesus Christ was/is in fact God come in the flesh, as the second person (if you will) of the Triune God head.

Important Biblical Definitions

1. '**Mar**': Meaning 'Master or Lord' in the Aramaic

2. '**Mari**': Also Aramaic meaning '…my LORD.'

3. '**Adon**': Hebrew meaning 'LORD.'

4. '**Adoni**': Meaning 'My LORD.'

5. '**YHVH or JHVH** the very sacred Tetragrammaton not a '*name*' meant to be spoken by the Hebrews ('Yes true there are transliterations such as Yehwah' or 'Jehovah' but strictly speculative. Actually the Watchtower has no scriptural right to use it as their name!) This unspoken Hebrew reference to God is used thorough out the Tanakh (Old Testament) over 6500 times. This is the eternal, memorial reference to Almighty God. Yah- the short version of YHVH (Yahweh) used in"hallelu-Yah (praise Yah), king Hezekiah (KhizqiYah Yah has strengthened), etc.

6. '**Yah**': The Aramaic short/or equal for the Tetragrammaton YHVH namely the God of Israel!

7. '**MarYah**': Contraction of 'Mar' and 'Yah' or 'Master/Lord Yah.'

8. '**Alaha' also transliterated 'Eloah**': Aramaic equivalent of the Hebrew 'Elohim' (the God of Israel).

9. '**Yeshua**': Yehoshua/Yeshua is the Hebrew name for Jesus. It means "Yahweh [**the Lord**] **is Salvation**." The English spelling of Yeshua is "Joshua." However, when translated from Hebrew into Greek, (in which the New Testament was written), Iesous **is** the Greek transliteration of the Hebrew name, and its English spelling **is** "Jesus.

Also it is important to remember that only part of the captive Jews left Babylon to return to Jerusalem after the 70 years of captivity, with the rest remaining in Babylon where Aramaic was the common language. 'MarYah' (Lord Yah) is used in both the Peshitta Aramaic N.T. and O.T. to be the *equal* of YHVH from the Hebrew Tanakh (O.T.).

'Yah' the Aramaic Short for the O.T
Hebrew Tetragrammaton 'YHVH'
The God of Israel the only True God!
Clearly Our Lord Jesus Is Spoken Of As Yeshua Meshikha MarYah Or Jesus Christ Lord God in the Aramaic Peshitta N.T.!

In order to better clarify the Biblical position on the Deity of our Lord Jesus Christ, I felt the need to contact one prolific in the original language concerning the Tetragrammaton. Roy Reinhold is responsible for a large part of this work. The following my letter to him and his educated critique on the JHVH or YHVH and the Aramaic Peshitta:

Brother Roy: Hello and God bless you. I am nearing the end of writing my new booklet on the Deity of Christ crystal clear in the Peshitta, but have a question you can answer. Question: "Does the Aramaic scripture ever have the Tetragrammation YHVH or JHVH ever in its pages written as those capital consonants???" If not then what was the exact Aramiac word used, as I think you said "Yah" was the short form for Yahweh which would be the reference to the Hebrew Tetragrammaton when it's translated into the Aramaic? Am I correct? The main question again is, "Is the JHVH or YHVH capital consonants ever used exactly as they are in the Aramaic Peshitta.

Brother Terry: No, the Peshitta Aramaic Tanach (Old Testament) translation involved a conscious decision to replace all 6500+ occurrences of the eternal memorial name of God--YHVH--with MarYah.

In my understanding, the completed Aramaic translation of the entire Hebrew Tanach was finished between 50 B.C. and 1 A.D.

The Peshitta Aramaic NT utilized the spoken language of the people in the land of Israel at the time of Yeshua/Jesus' ministry on the earth. There are 0 (zero) occurrences of YHVH in the Peshitta Aramaic NT. I just checked by doing a codes search of YHVH in the Peshitta Aramaic NT as a codes search text just now and there are no occurrences of YHVH in the text. MarYah is used throughout the Peshitta Aramaic NT and you have the verses for every occurrence that I gave to you. MarYah is the Aramaic cognate (substitute) for the Hebrew Yahweh (YHVH). Further, MarYah is the conflation of mar (Lord/Master) in Aramaic, and the name Yah which is the approved short version of Yahweh used in the Hebrew tanach and as part of the names of many prophets of Yahweh in the Hebrew Tanach and as part of the names of many prophets and kings. Elijah--actually Eli-Yah (my God is Yah) Jeremiah--actually Yerem--Yah (Yah will exalt; he will exalt as a verb with Yah being the subject) Netanyahu-- Netan--Yahu (gift of Yah)Mar in Aramaic is the equivalent of Adonai (my Lord/my Master) in Hebrew. Actually Adon is (lord/master) but used about God is Adonai.

So...the answer to your question is: No. MarYah is the Aramaic cognate (substitute) for Yahweh (YHVH) from the Hebrew scriptures. There are no occurrences of YHVH in either the Peshitta Aramaic Tanach or the Peshitta Aramaic NT. Likewise there are no occurrences of YHVH in the Greek Septuagint or Greek NT. The 72 scholars who translated the Hebrew Tanach to Greek for Pharaoh chose to substitute other terms for YHVH, thus not allowing Greeks to pronounce God's name Yahweh (YHVH) as revealed to the Hebrews. Roy Reinhold.

Further contact with brother Roy was needed to distinguish between YHVH and JHVH. Roy answered as following. (BTW Brother.

Reinhold can be contacted at his web site codes04@charter.net) Following is a comment by Rev. Bauscher, quite enlightening. (John 20).

> What is most interesting is the context of the passage, in which our resurrected Lord appears to Thomas, showing him his hands and side, and Thomas falls down and exclaims to Yesua: "My Lord and my God!"

27 ואמר לתאומא איתא צבעך להרכא וחזי אידי ואיתא אידך ואושט בגבי ולא תהוא לא מהימנא אלא מהימנא 28 וענא תאומא ואמר לה מרי ואלהי 29 אמר לה ישוע השא דחזיתני הימנת טוביהון לאילין דלא חזאוני והימנו 30 סגיאתא דין אתותא אחרניתא עבד ישוע קדם תלמידוהי אילין דלא כתיבן בכתבא הנא

Yud-Hey-Vav-Hey

Yud-Hey-Vav-Hey: The first letter is the consonant Y. The reason J came into use is through German to English. In German, the J is equivalent to the Y consonant and is pronounced soft and not hard J. English translators started using the German J and then over time English readers started using the J as a hard J by mistake. English translators of the Bible should have used the Y as a consonant for transliterated words. That's how Yeshua (Jesus) in German with soft J came into usage also. (BTW, God our Father and Yeshua our Messiah knows this and are not fuming over saying their name with a hard J). As far as how to pronounce YHVH, it is a problem that none of us will solve. There are groups who use Jehovah (they should say Yehovah), and most Christians use Yahweh. Few use Yahveh. In Hebrew there are two major groups of Hebrew speaking people--Ashkenazi from Northern Europe, Central Europe and Russia, and Sephardic who are Jews who lived in Arabic speaking nations across the world. In Arabic countries the vav is pronounced as a 'w'. In the USA, many professors of Hebrew are Sephardic trained while in Israel, Ashkenazi pronunciation is completely dominant (where vav as a consonant is v and not w). That's why academic publications in the USA lean heavily to usage of Arabic type pronunciations of Hebrew. I use Yahweh because it is the most used, so it is most comfortable for audiences. Actually I believe that YHVH is 3 syllables. Note Netanyahu, Eliyahu (long spelling of Elijah in the Bible), Yeremyahu (long spelling of Jeremiah in the Bible). Note all show the first 2 syllables of the pronunciation of YHVH--Yahu, yah-hoo. So the pronunciation grammatically would be Yah-hu-ah. Note if you say Yahuah fast it sounds like 2 syllables and sounds like Yahweh. :-) So...since the accepted academic usage is Yahweh, I suggest you use that. Note: Pastor Glenn Bauscher thinks Yehovah (Jehovah) is correct. Until God tells us, it is speculation from everyone. BTW, the I AM in Hebrew is "ehyeh" in Exodus 3:14 and the phrase is 'ehyeh asher ehyeh' (I AM that/who I AM).

Following note by brother Bauscher: I have found only three Bibles that use "Yahweh"- The Literal English Bible, Holman Christian Standard and New English Bible. I have found five that use "Jehovah" in some or all places for the Tetragrammaton -YHWH: KJV has it in a few places and "The LORD" in most places. Youngs Literal Translation has "Jehovah" in almost all 6800 places. Smith's Literal Translation has it as does ASV almost exclusively and the Darby Bible Translation. Every Hebrew Bible has the first and last vowel points Shewa, Qames for all but 50 occurrences of the name YHWH and no middle vowel. In 50 places, however, there is a middle vowel- Holem) long O). Those 50 preserve the full set of vowels for The Name. The title "Adonai" has the vowels, HatephPatheh (Heb. short a), Holem (o), Qames (a). "Ye-ho-vah'" Most scholars say that "Yehovah" was constructed by adding the vowels of "Adonai" to the 4 consonants -YHWH. This cannot be the case, since the first vowel of each word is different- "Shewa" in "Yehovah", and "HatephPatheh" in "Adonai."

Luke 2:11

A good starting point in the New Testament would be Luke 2:11. "For today is born to you in the city of David, a Savior, which is Christ the LORD (MarYah Meshikha, (i.e MarYah or LORD YHVH the Messiah). How incredibly important this is. Monumentally so! Plain declaration in the original Spirit of God, God breathed original New Testament manuscripts showing irrefutably that the babe born in the manger on that first Christmas day was none other than Almighty God, the second person of the trinity now clothed in human flesh! Plainly the body which the Spirit of God conceived, which was fully man (Yeshua/Jesus) and born to the virgin Mary, could be called 'the Son of God or literally 'God come in human form!'

Our Lord Jesus Christ was in every respect, 'God man,' or literally 'God come in the flesh! Absolutely two separate and distinct personalities encased in one body. So sad it is that when translated in the first century A.D. from the original God breathed Aramaic into Greek, that the Greek language while quite descriptive had no equal for the Tetragammaton in the translation of YHVH, and so the words 'Kurios (lord/master) and 'Theos' (God) were used in the Greek translation for the Tetragrammaton YHVH. The above verse clearly shows that the babe born in Bethlehem was/is YHVH (MarYah, Lord Yah the Messiah! We shall now go through the Peshitta Aramaic New Testament to find many other references to Jesus as to Him being (Kurios/LORD God come in the flesh.

Matthew 3:2-3

"Repent, for the kingdom of heaven is at hand. For this is the one referred to by Isaiah the prophet (40:3) saying, "The voice of one crying in the wilderness, make ready the way of the LORD (MarYah Yah=YHVH), make His paths straight." Mark 1:3, "The voice of one crying in the wilderness, make ready the way of the LORD (MarYah Yah=YHVH), make His paths straight." John 1:23 (John the Baptizer speaking), He said, "I am the voice of one crying in the wilderness, make straight the way of the LORD (MarYah, Yah=YHVH, Yahweh), the Messiah.

John the Baptist plainly knew that the coming Messiah was literally God coming in the form of human flesh! We have just seen above in Matthew 3:2-3 that John the Baptist fully identified the coming Messiah as the one Isaiah (40:3) had prophesied about. "The voice of one crying in the wilderness, make ready the way of the LORD (MarYah Yah=YHVH), make His paths straight." So...the coming Messiah was identified by Isaiah as MarYah=YHVH or the God of Israel coming in the flesh!

Matthew 4:7
Satan said to Jesus, "If thou be the Son of God, cast thyself down; for it is written, He shall give His angels charge concerning thee..." vs.7, Jesus said unto him, "It is written again thou shalt not tempt the Lord thy God." Again Satan said to Yeshua vs. 9, "All these things will I give thee if thou wilt fall down and worship me." Vs.10, Then Jesus said unto him, "Get thee hence, Satan: for it is written 'Thou shalt worship the Lord thy God and Him only shalt thou serve."

Here it is plain in the Aramaic Peshitta that our Lord told Satan, "Thou shalt not tempt the LORD MarYah (LORD Yah=YHVH) your God," and then "...for it is written 'Thou shalt worship the Lord thy God and Him only shalt thou serve.' In both instances it is crystal clear that Yeshua was speaking of Himself as being YHVH! Fact is the Greek word 'Kurios' (English 'Lord') in these several places was directly translated from the Aramaic 'Yah' equivalent of YHVH (LORD God) and directly from the Peshitta Aramaic. Again, MarYah is the Aramaic equivalent of the Hebrew Tetragrammaton.

John 8:10-11
Jesus said, "Woman, where are those thine accusers? Hath no man condemned thee? She said, No man, LORD (MarYah=Lord Yah=

YHVH). And Jesus said unto her, Neither do I condemn thee go and sin no more."

Note carefully Jesus did not rebuke the woman for referring to Him as (LORD) MarYah (YHVH or LORD Yah), because He indeed was God come in the flesh.

Matthew 21:9

And the multitudes that went before, and that followed, cried saying 'Hosanna to the Son of David: Blessed is he that cometh in the name of the LORD; Hosanna in the highest.'

Mr. Reinhold further points out as follows: "Hosanna is a conflation of two words, "hosha-na" in Hebrew, and in Aramaic "oshana." The Hebrew word "hosha" is a Hiphil imperative male singular word from the root word "yasha" (to save). The Hiphil is causative, so when they were saying "hosha-na" it should have been translated as "Cause me to be saved-please, O son of David" and "Cause me to be saved – please, in the Highest." This is a case of the translators just transliterating two Hebrew words and making them one very unusual coined word, point was they were saying that Yeshua on the donkey was MarYah (LORD Yah= YHVH)

Also note Matthew 23:39, "For I say to you from now on you shall not see Me until you say, "Blessed is He who comes in the name MarYah (LORD Yah=YHVH). Then Mark 11:9-10, "And those who went before, and those who followed after were crying out, "Hosanna, blessed is He who comes in the name (MarYah (LORD Yah= YHVH); blessed is the coming kingdom of our father David; Hosanna in the highest. Luke 13:35 "Behold, your house is left to you desolate; for I say to you , that you will not see Me until you say, Blessed is He who comes in the name MarYah (LORD Yah= YHVH)." Luke 19:38. (Triumphal Entry) "Blessed is He who comes in the name MarYah (LORD Yah=YHVH), peace in heaven and glory in the highest." John 12:13. (Triumphant Entry again). "…they took branches of the palm trees, and went out to meet Him, and began to cry out, 'Hosanna! Blessed is the King of Israel who comes in the name MarYah (LORD Yah= YHVH-Yahweh).

Luke 2:11
> "For unto you is born this day in the city of David a Savior, which is Christ the Lord."

Ian Michaels points out some very important truth found in this and related verses. Yeshua was confirmed to be our Savior by the angel in this verse. Now Ephesians 1:7 and Colossians 1:14 leave no doubt that only in Yeshua/Jesus is there found redemption and forgiveness of sin! Quoting, "In whom we have redemption through His blood even the forgiveness of sins." It is crystal clear the Lord Jesus/Yeshua went around forgiving sins without hesitation. See Mark 2:5-7, and Luke 5:21. Isaiah 43:3&11. Just who does the scripture declare is the long awaited Savior of the world? Yes, none other than Jesus our blessed (Mar Yah) Lord/God and Savior who not only forgives our sins as God the Son, but one who also was forecast in the Old Testament as the coming Savior of the world. Here the Word of God tells us that YHVH alone is our redeemer and as well He is the one saving and redeeming us!

1 Corinthians 12:3
> "…no man can say that Jesus is the Lord (MarYah/YHVH) but by the Holy Ghost."

No this verse is not using the term "Lord" (Aramaic to Greek 'Kurios' to English 'Lord' such as the Watchtower would have us believe such as 'lord' of a kingdom, but rather as the Almighty LORD GOD maker of heaven and earth! Remember the Greek had no equivalent for the Aramaic 'Yah'(which was the Tetragrammaton in Hebrew) so it was translated "Kurios"/Lord or "Theos"/God. BTW…Absolutely no one would be warned by the scripture here that Yeshua/Jesus could not be referred to as 'Lord' (i.e. 'Lord' of a kingdom only) unless by the power of the Spirit of God! Even those false theological systems who deny the Deity of our Savior have no qualms about referring to Jesus as 'Lord,' such as 'Lord of a Kingdom.' Paul therefore is plainly teaching that no man could say <u>that Yeshua//Jesus is the LORD God</u> unless revealed to him by the Spirit of God, and that is exactly what he meant. Indeed he was plainly teaching that Jesus/Yeshua MarYah was/is God almighty come in the flesh! Again, remember the Peshitta used the term 'Yah' short for YHVH the Hebrew Tetragrammaton referring only to God Almighty!

Psalm 110:1&5

The Lord said unto my LORD, Sit thou at my right hand until I make thine enemies thy footstool… Vs. 5, The Lord at thy right hand shall strike through kings in the day of His wrath.

Now this Psalm has David making a comment about 'his Lord' being spoken to by 'the LORD God Almighty concerning the fate of His (David's LORD's) enemies. In the Hebrew Tanach (Hebrew O.T.) the word 'LORD' in verse 5 originally was the \Tetragrammation but the Massorete scribe changed JHVH the Tetragrammaton from that to the Hebrew term 'Adonai' which yes, also refers to 'LORD'/God of the Hebrews. (This they did in 133 other places as well. So…Psalm 110 should have read, "The LORD God Almighty at thy right hand shall strike through kings in the day of His wrath…" So our LORD Jesus in quoting these verses to the Pharisees asked them just whose son the Messiah (Christ) was if he David called Him 'LORD.'

The Pharisees said the Messiah was the son of David, to which Jesus said "How can David then call Him LORD saying, (David saying) The LORD said unto my LORD, sit thou on my right hand till I make thine enemies thy footstool and if David then called Him LORD how is he his son? The importance of this is seen by the fact that here in Matthew Yeshua/Jesus is loudly proclaiming that the coming Messiah/Christ was shown to be literally God Almighty coming in the flesh!

The very sad thing to note here is that absolutely no Greek manuscript indicates this O.T. Divine 'Tetragrammaton'/(MarYah)YHVH the three times in these Matthew 22 verses but it DOES appear in the Aramaic Peshitta!! Also the Aramaic Peshitta names Yeshua/Jesus as 'Yah' (YHVH) about 29 more times in the rest of the N.T. Further it needs to be pointed out that the Greek only six times gives the deserved Aramaic title MarYah in translation as 'Kurios' or LORD in the (Greek) N.T. Also the other 239 times that MarYah/YHVH is referenced in quoting from the Hebrew O.T. are *not* translated as firm 'Deity' LORD GOD (Christ/Messiah) but rather 'Kurios' which as we know can refer to the Deity or to mere man. We of course do not here attempt to, or aim to denigrate the Greek Manuscripts, but merely show how that language did not have equal words to clearly indicate the Tetragrammaton in translation when it is needed. And yes the Greek manuscripts are perfectly clear that our Savior is literally God come in the form of man, to redeem the world from sin.

The Aramaic Peshitta 'MarYah' only refers to the Deity of Yeshua, and never mere man.

Chapter Nine

THE DIVINE 'YAH' OF THE N.T.

Exodus 3:13-14
And Moses said…I come unto the children of Israel…and I say…The God of your fathers hath sent me to you…and they say What is his name…what shall I say?…And God said unto Moses, I AM THAT I AM…say to the children of Israel, I AM hath sent me unto you.

Now this term in Hebrew means 'I AM' or "I AM THAT I AM." In the Aramaic this exact term for I AM is "Ena Na." In John's gospel this term(**Dr. I am adding since he more than deserves such title**) in the Peshitta Aramaic is used from the lips of Jesus/Yeshua about 23 times, and was such a powerful God breathed statement that when the soldiers came to arrest Jesus His use of this phrase "Ena Na" (John 18:6) forced them to fall to the earth. Our Savior as well used this phrase to Caiaphas the high priest when the priest demanded His true identity (Mark 14:62-63) "I AM THAT I AM" and the priest pointedly accused Yeshua/Jesus of blasphemy for making Himself equal with or literally God himself! It should be noted that the English translators of "Ena Na" usually added the italicized word 'he' after the I AM for better readability, but it was not in the original text. The term simply as 'I Am' brings with it more power to convey the Deity of Christ.

Acts 2:21

(Concerning the end times, Peter speaking), "And it shall be that everyone who calls on the name MarYah (LORD Yah= YHVH) shall be saved."

Acts 2:36

(Peter speaking). "Therefore let all the house of Israel know for certain that God has made this very Yeshua (Jesus) whom you have crucified, both MarYah (LORD Yah= YHVH) and the Messiah.

Acts 2:38

Then Peter said to them, "Repent and be baptized every one of you, in the name MarYah Yeshua (LORD Yah=YHVH) for the remission of sins, and ye shall receive the gift of the Holy Ghost." (d'Rudha d'Qudsha in Aramaic, Ruach Hakodesh in Hebrew).

Acts 5:14

"And believers were the more added to the LORD (MarYah, Lord Yah= YHVH) multitudes both of men and women."

Acts 9:5

Paul travelling on the road to Damascus had a vision of the Lord. "And he said, "Who art thou Lord, what wilt thou have me to do? And the LORD (MarYah, LORD Yah=YHVH) said unto him Arise and go into the city and it shall be told thee what thou must do."

Acts 9:27

But Barnabas took Him and brought Him to the apostles, and declared unto them how he had seen the LORD (MarYah Lord Yah=YHVH) in the way…"

Acts 10:36

Peter speaking, "For God sent the word to the children of Israel, preaching peace and tranquility by Yeshua the Messiah, He is MarYah (LORD Yah=YHVH) of all."

Acts 11:21

"And the hand of MarYah (LORD Yah-YHVH) who is Yeshua was with them; and a great number believed, and turned to MarYah."(LORD Yah =YHVH) who is Yeshua.

James 5:7

"Be patient therefore brethren unto the coming of the LORD MarYah (YHVH= Yeshua). Behold the husbandman waiteth for the precious fruit of the earth and hath long patience for it, until he receive the early and latter rain." (This is a prophecy of the MarYah (YHVH= Yeshua) coming to reign on the earth in the end times).

I Peter 3:15

But sanctify MarYah (LORD Yah or YHVH= Yeshua) in your hearts and be ready to give an answer in meekness and reverence to everyone who seeks from you a word concerning the hope of your faith.

Jude 1:14

And Enoch also the seventh from Adam prophesied of these, saying, Behold the LORD (MarYah-Yah=YHVH) cometh with ten thousands of His saints (*i.e. holy ones*), to execute judgment upon all… This is the end time coming of Yeshua to bring judgment on all the earth.

Romans 10:13

For whosoever shall call upon the name of the LORD (MarYah or YHVH=Yeshua) shall be saved.

Romans 14:9

For to this end Christ both died and rose and revived, that He might be LORD (MarYah or YHVH=Yeshua) both of the dead and living.

Romans 14:10-11

For we must all appear before the judgment seat of Christ (Messiah), for as it is written, As I live saith the LORD (MarYah or

YHVH=Yeshua= YHVH) every knee shall bow to me, and every tongue shall confess to God.

Romans 14:14
I know and am persuaded by the LORD (MarYah= Yeshua=YHVH) Jesus that there is nothing unclean of itself; but to him that esteemeth anything to be unclean to him it is unclean.

I Corinthians 4:4-5
For I know nothing by myself; yet am I not hereby justified; but he that judgeth me is the LORD (MarYah= Yeshua=YHVH). Therefore judge nothing before the time, until the LORD (MarYah=Yeshua=YHVH) come, who both will bring to light the hidden things of darkness and will make manifest the counsels of the hearts; and then shall every man have praise of God.

Here the return of the LORD Jesus/Yeshua is referred to bringing judgment on the world and clearly equates Yeshua to God the Father.

I Corinthians 8:6
But to us there is but one God the Father, of whom are all things and we in Him and one LORD (MarYah=Yeshua=YHVH) Jesus/Yeshua by whom are all things, and, and we by Him.

I Corinthians 11:27
Wherefore whosoever shall eat this bread and drink this cup of the LORD (MarYah=Yeshua=YHVH shall be guilty of the body and blood of the LORD (MarYah=Yeshua=YHVH.

I Corinthians 11:29
For he that eateth and drinketh unworthily, eateth and drinketh damnation to himself not discerning the LORD'S (MarYah=Yeshua=YHVH) body.

I Corinthians 15:47
The first man is of the earth, earthy; the second man is the LORD (MarYah=Yeshua=YHVH) from heaven. (*i.e. GOD come in human flesh to the earth!*)

I Corinthians 3:16-17
Nevertheless when it shall turn to the LORD (MarYah=Yeshua=YHVH), the fail shall be taken away. Now the LORD (MarYah=Yeshua=YHVH) is that Spirit and where the Spirit of the LORD (MarYah= Yeshua=YHVH) is, there is liberty.

Philippians 2:9-11
Wherefore God also hath highly exalted Him and given Him a name which is above every name; That at the name of Jesus every knee shall bow of things in heaven and things in earth and things under the earth; And that every tongue should confess that Jesus Christ is LORD (MarYah=Yeshua=YHVH) to the glory of God the Father.

Colossians 3:24
Knowing that of the Lord ye shall receive the reward of the inheritance for ye serve the LORD (MarYah=Yeshua=YHVH) Messiah.

We have just seen above in Matthew 3:2-3 that John the Baptist fully identified the coming Messiah as the one Isaiah (40:3) had prophesied about. "The voice of one crying in the wilderness, make ready the way of the LORD (MarYah Yah=YHVH), make His paths straight." The coming Messiah was identified by Isaiah as MarYah=YHVH or the God of Israel coming in the flesh!

Hebrews 13:6
So that we may boldly say, The Lord (MarYah= Yeshua=YHVH) is my helper and I will not fear what man shall do unto me. *Clearly it is being seen that in the epistles of Paul there is an extensive number of verses that clearly show the divinity of Yeshua in the Peshitta Aramaic*

NT (obscured in the Greek manuscripts) indicating that they (the Greek manuscripts) are a translation from the original Peshitta Aramaic NT).

Revelation 1:8

I am Alpha and Omega, the beginning and the ending saith the LORD. (MarYah=Yeshua=JHVH).

Reinhold comments: The same holds true *(the Aramaic Peshitta proclaiming the Deity of Christ)* for Revelation 21:6, 22:13, and 22:30." "…why is this important? There are over thirty specific N.T. examples tying Yeshua (Jesus) to the divine name of God…" Notice Isaiah 43:10-11. You are my witnesses, saith YHVH (Yahweh, MarYah in Aramaic) and my servant whom I have chosen in order that you may know and believe Me, and understand that I am He. Before Me there was no God formed, and there will be none after Me. I am I am YHVH (Yahweh, MarYah in Aramaic) and besides me there is no Savior. Isaiah 43:14 thus saith YHVH (Yahweh MarYah in Aramaic) Your Holy One, the Creator of Israel, your King. I could cite many more scriptures from the Tanakh showing that there is NO Savior, NO Redeemer, besides YHVH (Yahweh).

Further he states, "…the purpose of this paper is to show everyone that the Peshitta Aramaic New Testament clearly and decisively shows that MarYah=YHVH=Lord Yeshua Jesus Christ who is the Messiah and Savior. In Luke 19:38 and John 12:13 they cried out at the Triumphal Entry, "Hosanna! Blessed is the King of Israel who comes in the name MarYah (YHVH)." Isaiah 43:15 says that YHVH (MarYah) is the King of Israel, and Luke 19:38 and John12:13 confirms that in the Peshitta Aramaic NT, that it is MarYah Yeshua the Messiah.

Here is another odd and difficult verse for the Rabbis, and probably for many Christians as well. It is from the Songs of Moses and Israel, after Pharaoh and his army were drowned in the Sea of Suf. Exodus 15:2-4 Yah is my strength and song, and He has become my salvation. This is my God and I will praise Him; God of my father, and I will exalt Him. YHVH (Yahweh=MarYah in Aramaic) is a man of war. YHVH (Yahweh=MarYah in Aramaic) is His name. Pharaoh's chariots and his army He has thrown into the sea, and his chosen captains are drowned in the Sea of Suf.

The above verse is puzzling to my Jewish friends, since how could YHVH (Yahweh+MarYah in Aramaic) be a man and how could he be a man of war? God is not a man as everyone surmises. However the about 42 examples I cited in this article show that MarYah Yeshua the Messiah was YHVH; and that He was a man. Jude 1:14 is a prophecy about MarYah coming with ten thousands of His Holy Ones at the end of days (end-times). HE is coming as the Lion of Judah, a man of War. Are not the prophecies clear?

For example Zechariah 14:3-4 shows YHVH (MarYah) will go out and He will fight against those nations, as His day of fighting on a day of battle. And in that day His feet will stand on the Mount of Olives, which is in front of Jerusalem on the east; and the Mount of Olives will be split in its middle from east to west by a very large valley, so that half the mountain will move to the north and the other half to the south. YHVH (Yahweh, MarYah in Aramaic) will stand on the Mount of Olives with His own feet on the east side of Jerusalem.

This is MarYah Yeshua the Messiah who stands on Mount of Olives. The evidence is so blindingly clear, as shown that no one can deny it. What people can do is try to deny that the Peshitta Aramaic from the Greek manuscripts translated to English. MarYah Yeshua is not a conceptual Logos (Word of God) in His pre-natal existence as the Christadelphians and Watchtower witnesses claim. He was MarYah and the King of Israel from the beginning. He was not elevated to God status as the Arians, semi-Arians and Gnostics think-based on His successfully carrying out the crucifixion assignment. The evidence in this paper shows clearly that MarYah Yeshua was YHVH (Yahweh) before He came into the body as Yeshua some 2000 years ago! The evidence is in, are you willing to accept it? (You can contact the author, Roy at prophecy04@comcast.net.) Additional resources on the Peshitta Aramaic New Testament primacy: Andrew Gabriel Roth has two excellent books available that directly look at Peshitta primacy using specific verse examples. They can be obtained at: http://www.tushiyah.org Ruach Qadim: Aramaic Origins of the New Testament Ruach Qadim: The Path of life Andrews teaching website also has free articles on primacy (but not all the evidence in his books), and other Aramaic related articles at http://www.ruachqadim.com Pastor Bausher has many articles examining NT primacy using a number of scientific and linguistic methods (free). He also has completed a fresh new Bible translation-Interlinear and Plain English Bible-from the Peshitta Aramaic NT to English. Buy the Interlinear! His website is at http://aramaicnt.net

Chapter Ten

'BY THE MOUTH OF TWO OR THREE WITNESSES...'

Ian Michaels Further Uncovered the Following From His Article "What The Aramaic Reveals About Yshua Hanatzeret."
(Author note; I will not attempt to reproduce his work word for word, but will more or less summarize and condense it for the benefit of the reader/student. So...he certainly deserves full credit for the following material. In Mr. Michaels studies he points out the following scriptures which clearly show that Yeshua/Jesus is/was God come in the flesh.

John 18:6 Our Lord Jesus Told the Priest That His Idenity Was "Ena Na"

We have seen that this term comes from the Hebrew declaration of God to Moses at the burning bush that His name was 'I AM that I Am' and that name was what Moses was to tell the children of Israel of who sent him to deliver them. **Now this term in Hebrew is 'Ahiah' and means 'I AM' or 'Ahiah Asher and is the exact same meaning in the Aramaic as 'ENA NA.'** John's gospel contains these exact words 25 times, of which 23 came from the lips of Yeshua/Jesus!

Our Lord Jesus proclaiming His Deity. This term 'ENA NA' when used by our Lord seems to be somewhat confusing or obscure, but when it is used as He meant it to be understood the true sense is revealed. "So you may know that I am" or "Be not afraid" but when it is said "So that you may know that I am the living Elohim" or "Be not afraid, I am the living Elohim clears up the ambiguity. Remember the translators placed the italicized 'he' after those statements to make clearer readings in English etc., but not that it actually belonged there.

> **Readers note:** Ron Reinhold, Hebrew/Aramaic scholar corrects this above underlined statement. He tells us that it should be pronounced "ehyeh asher ehyeh." This is the correct pronunciation and the transliteration should be Ehyeh asher Ehyeh or "I AM that I AM." He further states that it is important to be correct here since this is a name of God.

Matthew 1:23/Isaiah 7:14
Behold a virgin shall conceive and she shall bear a son and they shall call his name Emmanuel which is translated "with us is Alaha." Remember 'Alaha' is the Aramaic equivalent of the Hebrew YHVH or Elohim! Plainly Yeshua/Jesus is/was God come in the flesh.

Matthew 4:7, Luke 4:12
Yeshua said to him, "Again it is written, "You shall not tempt MarYah your Alaha.

Matthew 14:27, Mark 6:50, John 6:20
And He said, "Take heart, ENA NA (or **I am the living Elohim** while the actual English translations say merely "I am *he*.") Do not be afraid.

Matthew 24:5 Mark 13:6, Luke 21:8
For many will come in my name, and they will say, 'Ena Na (I am the living Elohim, the Messiah.' According to the ancient Hebraic understanding, a declaration of Messiahship is equal to a declaration of Divinity.

Luke 2:11

For unto you this day in the city of David, a Savior which is MarYah Meshikha."

This is one of the most amazing of statements in the Gospels, and probably the first unequivocal revelations of the Deity of Yeshua. MarYah Meshikha means YHWH the Messiah, and this declaration is being made by the angel from heaven.

Luke 3:4 Mark 1:3, John 1:23

Just as it is written in the book of the words of Isaiah the prophet which says, 'The voice which cries in the wilderness "Prepare the way of MarYah and straighten in the plain a road for our Alaha.'

John 1:1

Mr. Michaels has gone to the original Aramaic to give the exact message of this powerful verse, much more so than in the English version as follows: "In the origin, Miltha (the manifestation) had existed and that Miltha had existed with Alaha and that Miltha was Himself Alaha."

John 1:18

No man has seen Alaha at any time: The only begotten Alaha who is in the bosom of the father, He has declared Him. (In the Peshitta Alaha meaning 'The only begotten Son can account for the variant Greek readings monogenais Theos or 'the only begotten Elohim and monogenais uios (the only begotten Son) the Aramaic text can mean 'only begotten Elohim' or 'only begotten Son of Elohim.'

John 4:26

Yeshua said to her, Ena Na (I am the living Elohim) who am speaking with you.

John 5:18
Therefore the Jews sought the more to kill him, because He not only had broken the Sabbath but said also that God/Elohim was His Father making himself equal with God/Alaha.

John 6:35,48
Yeshua said to them, 'Ena Na (I am the living Elohim), the bread of life, whoever comes to Me will not hunger, and whoever trusts in me will never thirst.'

John 6:51
'Ena Na (I am the Living Elohim) the Living Bread who came down from heaven and if a man will eat of this bread, he will live forever and the bread that I shall give is my body that I give for the sake of the life of the world.'

John 8:10-11
But when He stood up, Yeshua said to the woman, "Where are they?" Has no man condemned you? But she said, "Not even one MarYah, and Yeshua said, even I am not condemning you. Go and from now on sin no more. (This text reveals a very powerful testimony from the woman taken in adultery. She addressed Yeshua with the Divine Name 'MaryYah" This would indicate that the Holy Spirit had revealed our Messiah's identity to her, and that she was instantly saved/born again since according to the Scripture; "…no one can say Yeshua is MarYah except by the Holy Spirit. See 1 Cor. 12:3."

John 8:12
Ena Na (I am the living Elohim) the light of the world, he that follows me shall by no means walk in darkness, but shall find the light of life.

John 8:12
Ena Na (I am the living Elohim) the light of the world, he that follows me shall by no means walk in darkness but shall find the light of life.

John 8:18
Ena Na (I am the living Elohim) that bears witness of myself and the Father that sent me bears witness of me.

John 8:24
If you do not believe that Ena Na (I am the living Elohim) you shall die in your sins. This is one of the places where the Greek texts have the phrase 'ego'(the Being for Ena Na, English versions insert the italicized word 'He' to make sense of the stand alone 'I AM' at the end of the phrase.)

John 8:28
When you have lifted up the son of Man, then you will know that Ena Na (I AM the Living Elohim)... (Again the **Being** in Greek and the italicized **'he'** to make sense of the stand alone 'I AM at the end of the phrase in English...)

John 8:58
Verily Verily I say unto you, before Abraham was born, Ena Ithay. (This phrase is a variant of Ena Na and is equal to the Hebrew phrase recorded in Exodus 3:4 &14 when YHWH spoke to Moses from the burning bush saying **Asher High/I Am that I Am**.

> **Readers note:** Ron Reinhold, Hebrew/Aramaic scholar again corrects this above underlined statement (by Mr. Michaels). He tells us that it should be pronounced "ehyeh asher ehyeh." This is the correct pronunciation and the transliteration should be Ehyeh asher Ehyeh or "I AM that I AM." He further states that it is important to be correct here since this is a name of God.

John 10:7 & 9B
Verily verily I say unto you, Ena Na (I am the Living Elohim) the door of the sheep...by me if any man go in he shall find life and shall go in and out and find pasture.

John 10:11
Ena Na (I Am the living Elohim) the Good Shepherd; the Good Shepherd gives His life for the sheep.

John 10:14
Ena Na (I am the Living Elohim) the Good Shepherd and know my sheep and am known of mine.

John 10:33
The Judeans were saying to him, It is not for excellent works that we are stoning you for, but for blasphemy and as you are a man you make yourself Alaha (Aramaic for Elohim/God).

John 11:25
Yeshua/Jesus told her Ena Na (I Am the Living Elohim) the resurrection and the life and whoever believes in Me even though they be dead shall live.

John 13:19
Now I am telling you before it happens, that when it has occurred, you may believe Ena Na (I am the Living Elohim). This is yet another place where the Greek texts have 'The Being) and English texts add the 'he' to the 'I Am' that stands alone at the end of the phrase. Several times Yeshua tells the disciples that they shall believe 'Ena Na' (I Am). They apparently had not yet believed in His absolute Deity until after His death and resurrection. So sublime and deep is the significance of these words, that they were seldom understood or even heard by those to whom He spoke them. There are 150 occurences of this term in 10 books of the Peshitta OT, 147 of which are utterances of the Deity. No other text besides the Peshitta properly sets forth this claim of our Master Yeshua Meshikha as plainly. Along with the 32 times the title MarYah (YHWH is applied to Yeshua Meshikha, there are counting the 25 Ena Na statements in John, 57 very powerful tes-

timonies to the absolute Deity of the Messiah Yeshua in the Peshitta NT not found in other Bible Texts.

John 14:6
Yeshua said to him, Ena Na (I am the living Elohim) the Way the Truth and the Life, no man comes to my Father but by me.

John 15:1
Ena Na (I am the living Elohim) the True Vine and my Father is the vine dresser.

John 15:5
Ena Na (I am the Living Elohim) the Vine and you are the branches; whoever abides with Me and I in him, this one brings forth much fruit, because without me, you can do nothing.

John 18:6
And when Yeshua said to them, Ena Na (I am the living Elohim) they went backwards and fell to the ground.

John 18:8
Yeshua said to them, I have told you that Ena Na (I am the living Elohim) and if you are seeking Me let these men go.

John 20:28
And Thomas answered and said to Him, My Master and my Alaha (Aramaic for Elohim or Almighty God).

Acts 2:36
Let therefore the whole house of Israel know truly, Alaha (Aramaic for Elohim) has made this Yeshua MarYah and Meshikha (the Messiah) whom you had crucified.

Acts 2:38

And Simeon said to them. Return to Alaha (Elohim) and be immersed every one of you in the name of MarYah (YHVH) for the forgiveness of sins, so that you may receive the gift of the Holy Spirit.

Acts 9:4-5

And he fell upon the ground and heard a voice which said to him, Saul Saul why do you persecute me? It is hard for you to kick against the pricks. He answered and said, Who are you my Master? And the Master said, Ena Na (I am the living Elohim) Yeshua the Nazarene whom you are persecuting.

Acts 9:27

But Barnabas took Saul and brought him to the Apostles and he related just how he had seen MarYah on the road and that he had spoken with him on the road, and in Damascus he had spoken openly in the name of Yeshua.

Acts 10:36

For the word which he sent to the children of Israel and announced good news of peace and tranquility to them by Yeshua the Messiah! This one is MarYah of all.

Acts 18:9

And MarYah said in a vision to Paul, "Do not be afraid, but speak and do not be silent…(it was Yeshua that Saul {also called Paul in the Peshitta} was seeing in the vision).

Acts 20:28

Give heed to your selves therefore and to the whole flock which the Holy Spirit has appointed you overseers, to the shepherd/feed the church of Alaha (God) which He has purchased with His own blood.

Romans 14:9

For this purpose also the Messiah died and lived and arose that he would be MarYah to the dead and to the living. (The Messiah is YHWH according to the Peshitta, which so names Him nearly 60 times. The first time He was announced to be so upon the earth was by an angle from heaven Luke 2:8-11.

Romans 14:10

But why are you judging your brother, or why do you even despise your brother for all of us are going to stand before the judgment seat of Meshikha. (In this passage the critical Greek text translates 'Messiah' as Theos (Greek for 'God').

Romans 14:14

For I know and am persuaded by MarYah Yeshua that there is nothing unclean of itself...

1 Corinthians 8:6

But to us there is but one God the Faather of whom are all things and we in Him and one MarYah Yeshua Meshikha by whom are all things and we by Him.

1 Corinthians 11:27

Wherefore whosoever shall eat this bread and drink this cup of MarYah unworthily shall be guilty of the body and blood of MarYah. (See also Acts 20:28). The divine sense in the Greek here is somewhat lost due to the fact that the Greek has no equivalent for the sacred name MarYah. All Greek texts have 'kurios' or Lord for MarYah so the import could be taken correctly as 'Elohim' or mistaken for 'lord' king or human dignitary.

1 Corinthians 11:29
For he that eateth and drinketh unworthly, eateth and drinketh damnation to himself not discerning the body of MarYah.

1 Corinthians 12:3
Wherefore I give you to understand that no man speaking by the Spirit of Alaha calleth Yeshua accursed and that no man can say that Yeshua is MarYah but by the Holy Spirit.

Philippians 2:5-6
Let this mind be in you which was also in Meshikha who being in the form of Alaha thought it not robbery to be equal with Alaha.

Philippians 2:11
And that every tongue should confess that Yeshua Meshikha is MarYah to the glory of Alaha His father. (The Name higher than all names is MarYah ('LORD YHWH') the Aramaic cognate of the Hebrew OT Name YHWH or the name of Elohim,. The Greek texts have merely Kurios which is not the highest name in the Greek, as it is not a name at all, merely a title which is used for landowners, merchants/ nobles and also is used in Greek and by Greeks for some pagan deities, as well at times is correctly used for Elohim of Israel.

Colossians 3:24
Knowing that of the Lord (YHVH MarYah, Greek has Kurious or 'Lord') ye shall receive the reward of the inheritance for ye serve the MarYah/Meshikha. (…or YHVH the Messiah. This is identical to the first announcement of Yeshua's divinity upon the earth made by the angel from heaven in Luke 2:11.

Titus 2:13
Looking for that blessed hope and the glorious appearing of the great Alaha and our Saviour Yeshua Meshikha.

Chapter Eleven

Thankfully Notice the Watchtower Unwitting Translation!

Titus 2:13-14
"While we wait for the happy hope and glorious manifestation of the great God and of our Savior, Jesus Christ, **14** who gave himself for us to set us free from every sort of lawlessness and to cleanse for himself a people who are his own special possession, zealous for fine works." N.W.T. *(Notice here they are forced by unwitting factual translation to admit Jesus/Yeshua is indeed the same as Almighty God!)*

Further Peshitta Proof Texts Yeshua Is God

Hebrews 1:8-9/Psalm 45:6-7
But unto the Son He saith, Thy throne O Alaha, is forever and ever a scepter of righteousness is the scepter of thy kingdom. Thou hast loved righteousness and hated iniquity, there Alaha, even thy Alaha hath anointed thee with the oil of gladness above thy fellows. And Thou MarYah in the beginning hast laid the foundation of the earth and the heavens are the works of thine hands.

Thy throne O Alaha is forever and ever the scepter of thy kingdom is a right scepter. Thou lovest righteousness and hatest wickedness therefore Alaha thy Alaha hath anointed thee with the oil of gladness above thy fellows.

Hebrews 2:9
But we see Yeshua who was made a little lower than the angels for the suffering of death, crowned with glory and honour that He (Alaha) by the grace of Alaha, should taste death for every man.

James 5:7
Be patient therefore brethren unto the coming of MarYah, behold the husbandman waiteth for the precious fruit of the earth…

1 Peter 3:15
But sanctify MarYah Meshikha in your hearts, and be ready always to give an answer to every man that asketh you…

John 5:20
And we know that the Son of Alaha is come and hath given us an understanding that we may know Him that is true and we are in Him that is true even in His Son Yeshua Meshikha. This is the true Alaha and Eternal Life.

Revelation 1:7-8
Behold He cometh with clouds and every eye shall see Him and they also which pierced Him, and all kindreds of the earth shall wail because of Him. Even so Amen. I am Alpha and Omega the beginning and the ending saith MarYah Alaha which is and which was and which is to come. (The Alpha and the Omega is equal to the "first and the last" which YHWH calls Himself in Isaiah 41:4, 44-6, and 48:12. Yeshua says this twice in this book here and Revelation 22:13.

Revelation 4:8
And the four beasts had each of them six wings about Him and they were full of eyes within and they rest not day and night saying, Holy, Holy, Holy MarYah Alaha Almighty. (MarYah occurs 14 times as

such in this manuscript of Revelation. The first is 1:8 and the last is 22:20 where Yeshua is addressed as MarYah Yeshua.

Revelation 22:16
I Yeshua have sent mine angel to testify unto you these things in the churches. Ena Na (I am the living Elohim) the root and the offspring of David and the bright morning star.

Revelation 22:20
He which testifieth thse things saith Surely I come quickly. Amen. Even so come MarYah Yeshua.

Jesus/Yeshua Receives Worship As Only God Can Proving He Is JHVH or the Almighty Creator God of the Universe

The false Watchtower claim that John 1:1 should have the definite article 'a' in front of 'GOD' making Jesus merely 'a god' totally falls apart when the scriptures are closely examined. One thing stands out to begin with is that in verse 14 'the Word' was manifest in the flesh and is clearly identified as none other than the blessed Savior the Lord Jesus Christ. Watchtower, and nearly every religious group this author knows of (who embrace the Old and New Testaments as being divinely inspired), believes in the pre-existence of Jesus in the heavens before He came to earth being born of the Virgin Mary. Thus it comes down to only one of two possibilities concerning the identity of Yeshua. Either He was indeed the second personage of the Trinity (Watchtower adamantly reject the doctrine of the Trinity) taking the form of human flesh, or He was a created being, created by Elohim/God Almighty as an inferior being or literally an angelic/angel being. Certainly He could not be both. The Watchtower categorize Him as merely 'a god' created by the Almighty, and given the power to do His father's creating of all things that exist, whether in heaven or earth or under the earth.

Colossians 1:16
For by Him were all things created that are in heaven and that are upon earth visible and invisible, whether thrones, or dominions, or principalities or powers all things were created by Him and for Him.

Now the gigantic problem with the idea that the Almighty God gives the inferior 'god' (*Watchtower claim that 'inferior 'god is Jesus*) the identical powers which He has in order to do the all of creation for Him is seen in the three Omni's of Almighty God. They are Omnipotence or all Power, Omnipresence, or all Presence, and Omniscient or all knowing. For the Almighty to give the 'smaller lesser 'god' the same Omni's which He irrefutably holds, is to create a second Almighty God equal to Himself! Doing such clearly contradicts His own word as follows.

(*Interesting note:* If the one and only JHVH Almighty God were to 'create' another 'God' equal to Himself in every way, then the Watchtower should have no problem believing in the Trinity or a Triune God! By their saying that the All powerful God YHVH gave their lesser 'god' of John 1:1 equality with Himself they are one step away from believing in a Triune God head!)

Isaiah 45:5-6, 12, 14-15, 18
I am the Lord, and there is none else, there is no God besides me…I am the Lord and there is none else…I form the light and create the darkness…I have made the earth and created man upon it, I even my hands have stretched out the heavens, and all their host have I commanded…Verily thou art a God that thou hidest thyself O God of Israel, the Savior…For thus saith the Lord that created the heavens, God himself that formed the earth and made it, He hath established it, He created it not in vain,, He formed it to be inhabited, I am the Lord and there is none else. K.J.V.

> **Readers note:** Mr. Reinhold points out that the K.J.V. English translation (above) is not as clear as needs be in showing Yeshua as MarYah or Yahweh. So following he gives the correct rendering of this verse from the original languages mirrored by the correct English. (Brilliantly so.)

I am Yahweh(LORD, MarYah), and there is none, there is no God besides me...I am Yahweh (LORD, MarYah) and there is none else...I form the light and create the darkness...I have made the earth and created man upon it, I even my hands have stretched out the heavens, and all their host have I commanded...Verily thou art a God that thou hidest thyself O God of Israel, the Savior...For thus saith the Lord that created the heavens, God himself that formed the earth and made it, He hath established it, He created it not in vain,, He formed it to be inhabited, I am Yahweh(LORD, MarYah) and there is none else.

Again...notice the K.J.V. 1611
I am Yahweh(LORD, MarYah), and there is none, there is no God besides me...I am Yahweh (LORD, MarYah) and there is none else...I form the light and create the darkness...I have made the earth and created man upon it, I even my hands have stretched out the heavens, and all their host have I commanded...Verily thou art a God that thou hidest thyself O God of Israel, the Savior...For thus saith the Lord that created the heavens, God himself that formed the earth and made it, He hath established it, He created it not in vain,, He formed it to be inhabited, I am Yahweh(LORD, MarYah) and there is none else.

So here we must pause and look back at Colossians 1:16 for absolute clarification and see how the two portions of scripture compliment, not contradict each other... It cannot be plainer that there is one and only one Almighty God, not two, three or four. But yea, one God manifested in three persons! We must add here that this above verse in Isaiah chapter 45 clearly and irrefutably identifies who the Savior of Israel (and the whole world) really is, and that is Yeshua/Jesus or the Word of God come in the flesh! Yeshua was literally 'God himself come in the flesh.

Colossians 1:16
For by Him were all things created that are in heaven and that are upon earth visible and invisible, whether thrones, or dominions, or principalities or powers all things were created by Him and for Him.

Of course there will be someone who will use this truth (one God manifested in three persons) to claim Christians believe in a Trinity which they say is really believing in a plurality of three separate Almighty "Gods." That is absolutely false. We who believe the Bible see God revealed as One God but that one God is manifested in three separate and distinct personages, God the Father, God the Son (the Word who is the personification of JHVH's spoken Word), and God the Holy Spirit. A trinity or trinity truth is manifested in nature, when we have H20 we can see it manifested in three separate and distinct characters, water, steam and ice. The same with the sun, one sun, but manifested in three characters, light, heat, and chemical energy. When John 1:1 speaks of Yeshua/Jesus as being 'the Word' of God, it is plain that when Almighty God spoke everything into existence it was our Savior the Lord Jesus Christ the Word of God who was speaking creation. Maybe better said literally Almighty God Himself speaking everything into existence, visible and invisible, yea all things into existence! No! Our Savior was not 'given' His powers from Almighty God (as 'a 'god…Watchtower false translation claim), but was the second person of the blessed trinity God the Word the Creator of all things, visible and invisible.

Chapter Twelve

JESUS ACCEPTS DIVINE WORSHIP AS YHVH/JHVH

Our Lord Jesus Openly Receives Worship Which Worship Can Only Be Deserved By Almighty God Showing He was Indeed God Come In The Flesh!

Hebrews 1:5-14

For which of the angels said he at any time, Thou art my Son, this 'day have I begotten (*ed. 'begotten 'speaking of the Divine creative/ conception by the Spirit of God of the physical body of our Savior, and remember this was not creation of our Savior as He was already pre-existent in eternity past as second member of the Triune God head. Being 'begotten 'merely refers to the creation by God/Elohim of the Divinely conceived embro in the womb of the virgin Mary and thus making Yeshua the Son and Elohim the Father*) thee? And again I will be to Him a Father and He shall be to me a Son? And again when He bringeth in the first begotten into the world He saith, And let all the angels of God worship Him. And of the angels He saith Who maketh His angels spirits and His ministers a flame of fire, but unto the Son He saith, Thy throne o God is forever and ever a scepter of righteousness is the scepter of thy kingdom. Thou hast loved righteousness and hated iniquity, therefore God, even thy God hath anointed thee with the oil of gladness above thy fellows. And Thou Lord in the beginning hast laid the foundation of the earth and the heavens are the works of thine hands. They shall perish, but thou remainest and they all shall wax old as doth a garment and as vesture shalt thou fold them up and they shall be changed but thou art the same and thy years shall not fail. But to which of the angels said He at any time Sit on my right hand until I make thine enemies thy footstool? Are they not all ministers for them who shall be heirs of salvation?

YHVH Almighty God Verbally Gives Recognition of the Deity of Yeshua His Only Begotten Son as the Creator of All There Is

1. Notice first Yeshua is revealed as full Deity as His body was conceived supernaturally by YHVH and the pre-incarnate Word was encased in that fleshly body, as John said, "And the Word became flesh and dwelt among us." Jn. 1:14.

2. John 1:1 does not say that the "Word" was an angel and the angel became flesh…but that the "Word was God and (vs. 14) the Word became flesh and dwelt among us." Jesus was literally "God come in the flesh." Certainly a devastatingly blow to Watchtower doctrine.

3. God JHVH calls upon the angels to worship His only begotten son. Angels are not to worship angels. They were commanded to worship the Word who had come in the flesh!

4. Not only that, but two times in the above verses JHVH calls Yeshua/Jesus GOD, and one time LORD!

5. Then the absolute recognition of Yeshua/Jesus being the one as the Word of God being the all powerful creator of the entire universe, all there is or ever will be. He said "And Thou Lord in the beginning hast laid the foundation of the earth and the heavens are the works of thine hands."

(*Interesting note:* If the one and only JHVH Almighty God were to 'create' another 'God' equal to Himself in every way, then the Watchtower should have no problem believing in the Trinity or a Triune God! By their saying that the All powerful God YHVH gave the 'god' of John 1:1 equality with Himself they are one step away from correctly believing in a Triune God head!)

Following From the Poorly Translated Watchtower Version These Very Important Hebrew Verses Still Prove the Diety of Our Savior!

For example, to which one of the angels did God ever say: "You are my son; today I have become your father"? And again: "I will become his father, and he will become my son"? But when he again brings his Firstborn into the inhabited earth, he says: "And let all of God's angels do obeisance to him." Also, he says about the angels: "He makes his angel's spirits and his ministers a flame of fire." But about the Son, he says: "God is your throne forever and ever, and the scepter of your Kingdom is the scepter of uprightness. You loved righteousness, and you hated lawlessness. That is why God, your God, anointed you with the oil of exultation more than your companions." And: "At the beginning, O Lord, you laid the foundations of the earth, and the heavens are the works of your hands. They will perish, but you will remain; and just like a garment, they will all wear out, and you will wrap them up just as a cloak, as a garment, and they will be changed. But you are the same, and your years will never come to an end." But about which of the angels has he ever said: "Sit at my right hand until I place your enemies as a stool for your feet"? Are they not all spirits for holy service sent out to minister for those who are going to inherit salvation?

Critical Note on 'Obeisance' in Reference to Our Lord

Now the question looms "Why is the Watchtower translation translating the Greek 'Proskuneo' as 'obeisance' as above instead of by 'worship' as the KJV (etc.) does? The answer as follows.

In the NWT, every time the Greek word "proskuneo" is used in reference to God, it is translated as "worship" (Rev 5:14, 7:11, 11:16, 19:4, Jn 4:20, etc.). Every time "proskuneo" is used in reference to Jesus, it is translated as "obeisance" (Mt 14:33, 28:9, 28:17, Lk 24:52, Heb 1:6, etc.), even though it is the same word in the Greek (see Gr-Engl Interlinear).

Especially compare the Greek word "prosekunhsan" used with reference to God in Rev 5:14, 7:11, 11:16, and 19:4 and used with reference to Christ in Mt 14:33, 28:9, and 28:17. What is the reason for this inconsistency? If the NWT was consistent in translating "proskuneo" as "worship", how would the verses above referring to Christ read?

Conclusion

1. The Greek term 'proskuneo' when used in reference to God or Deity is translated as 'worship.'

2. When it is used in reference to a mortal, king, emperor etc (non deity) it is translated as 'obeisance.'

3. The Watchtower does not believe our Lord Jesus was God come in the flesh, so they translated proskuneo as 'obeisance.'

4. Hebrews 1:5-14 clearly identifies our Lord Jesus Christ as "God" as being addressed as such (God) by His Father. I.e. God the incarnate Son of God being addressed by His Father as exact equal, literally 'God.'

In Christianity, worship is the act of attributing reverent honor and homage to God. In the New Testament, various words are used to refer to the term worship. One is proskuneo ("to worship") which means to bow down to God or kings. ... Orthodoxy in faith also meant orthodoxy in worship, and vice versa: [5]

Luke 4 Our Lord Jesus As God Rebuking Satan
In these verses, 1-13 we see our LORD Jesus using the truth of His Deity to rebuke Satan! Satan calling upon Jesus our Lord to 'do obeisance to him, or literally to 'worship' him, and he would give Him all the kingdoms of the world, but Jesus said, "Get thee behind me Satan for it is written thou shalt worship the LORD thy God and

Him only shalt thou serve." Vs. 8. Simply put, Jesus was saying, "No, I'll not worship you, you are to worship me."

Next in verses 9-12 Satan challenges our Lord to test the scriptures which would protect Him from harm if He was indeed the Son of God. This challenge actually is Satan tempting our Lord to obey him in doing such an action. Our Lord could not obey Satan since to obey him was to obey a temptation conceived of the Devil, who is a liar and the father of it, and thus commit sin. Not only that but by our Lord to respond to such a thing, would be for Him to show doubt that He was who He really claimed to be, God the Son, or perhaps He needed to prove the validity of His Father's promised protection. (God His Father could not fail to keep His word!) Here again our Lord Jesus/Yeshua was saying "I am the Lord your God and you are not to tempt/test Me. Another thing to consider is that for our Lord to have done such would have been a foolish, irresponsible thing to do. To be sure Jesus could or would do nothing foolish, and as well such would have been outside the will of God, which He well knew! Perhaps also, the protective scriptures relating to the Messiah our Lord, no doubt were to be enacted by the angels when and only when our Lord inadvertently came into danger, not when He deliberately placed Himself in a harmful situation outside of the will of His Father. The thought has come to this author that since Satan is not omniscient (all knowing) then the wilderness temptation could as well be the only time the Devil was actually attempting to violate our Lord's sinlessness, Satan not knowing for sure the purity of the incarnation, since a human physical body was now a part of the person of Yeshua, God the Son. Our Lord was at the beginning of His ministry, and certainly Satan was not agreeable to God's only begotten Son coming into his earthly kingdom to begin the ministry of overthrowing his evil powers. Thus a futile attempt to cause Jesus to sin.

Clearly our Lord Jesus as the only begotten Son of His Father YHVH could be nothing less than fully equal with Him in every respect. Like begets like, so truly Jesus was literally God the Word, the second person of the Trinity come in the flesh! Next we see…

Jesus coming in the clouds mounted on a white horse speaking the wrath of Almighty God with the two edged sword and on his vesture…the titles of Deity!

Revelation 19:15
And out of His mouth goeth a sharp sword, that with it He should smite the nations and He shall rule them with a rod of iron and He treadeth the winepress of the fierceness and wrath of Almighty God and He hath on his vesture and on His thigh a name written KING of Kings and LORD of Lords.

I am quite sure that when this is considered, i.e. the clear unmistakable titles of Deity clearly emblazoned on this rider's thigh, that those who deny the Deity of Christ, will say 'Well the rider on this white horse only had these titles in order to prove to the world that Almighty God was the one sending Him forth to war. Of course who ever says such, shows his own ignorance of scripture. Going back to verse 13 He is clearly identified.

Revelation 19:13
And He was clothed with a vesture dipped in blood and His name is called, "The Word of God!"

This revelation was first revealed in John 1:1, In the beginning was the Word and the Word was with God and the Word was God! Yes certainly our LORD Jesus/Yeshua was/is clearly the KING of Kings and LORD of Lords. Verily Almighty God! Clearly proclaimed in verse 8 of Revelation chapter 1. Plainly when He is proclaimed 'LORD OF Lords' then He cannot be 'a god' who was 'created' by an Almighty God above Him as the Watchtower falsely teach.

Here again we must for the sake of truth, go back to the first chapter of Revelation verses 4-8.

Revelation Chapter 1:4-8

John to the seven churches which are in Asia; Grace be unto you and peace from Him which is, and which was, and which is to come; and from the seven Spirits which are before His throne; And from Jesus Christ who is the faithful witness and the first begotten of the dead, and prince of the kings of the earth. Unto Him that loved and washed us from our sins in His own blood. And hath made us kings and priests unto God and His father; to Him be glory and dominion forever and ever Amen. Behold He cometh with clouds; and every eye shall see Him and they also which pierced Him and all kindreds of the earth shall wail because of Him. Even so Amen I am Alpha and Omega the beginning and the ending saith the LORD, which is, and which was and which is to come **the Almighty.**

1. Quite a number of things here which identifies our Lord Jesus as 'Almighty God.' Acts 20:28 tells us: Take heed therefore unto yourselves and to all the flock over which the Holy Ghost hath made you overseerers to feed the church of God which He hath purchased **with His own blood**. It cannot be denied the blood of Jesus is referred to as 'the blood of God.'

2. Here Jesus is plainly referred to as the First and the Last, the Beginning and the Ending, the Alpha and Omega, i.e. none or nothing before Him and nothing can be after Him, only possible for the Lord God to say. Clearly only Almighty God can be said to be 'first and last and the beginning and the end!'

3. Then following He who is the Alpha and Omega title is the clear title given to Jesus as "The Almighty. (vs.8) certainly as the scripture plainly says, He thought it not robbery to be equal with God! Philippians 2:5-6. Let this mind be in you which was also in Christ **Jesus who being in the form of God** thought it not robbery **to be equal with God.**

4. Even more powerful is Genesis 1:1, "In the beginning <u>God</u> created the heavens and the earth…" Our Lord Jesus was one of the triune God head in eternity past, exercising his omnipotence (all power) in **creating all that there is, invisible and visible.** Col. 1:14-16,. "In whom we have redemption through His blood, even the forgiveness of sins. Who is the image of the invisible God, the firstborn of every creature For by Him were all things created that are in heaven and that are in earth, visible, and invisible whether they be thrones or dominions, or principalities or powers, **all things were created by Him and for Him.** Clearly our Savior the Lord Jesus Christ was every bit God Almighty in His pre-incarnate form!

Titus 1:2-3 and 2 Peter 1:1

In hope of eternal life which God that cannot lie promised before the world began: but hath in due times manifested His word through preaching which is committed unto me according to the commandment of <u>God our Savior</u>. (Titus). (K.J.V)

Notice how close the N.W.T. is to our A.V.

In hope of eternal life, which God, that cannot lie, promised before the world began. But hath in due times manifested his word through preaching, which is committed unto me according to the commandment of **God our Savior**; Titus 1:2-3.

Simon Peter a servant and an apostle of Jesus Christ to them that have obtained like precious faith with us through the righteousness of God and our Savior Jesus Christ. 2 Peter 1:1-2

Notice now how close the N.W.T. Watchtower translation is to the King James version (2 Peter 1:1):

> Simon Peter, a slave and an apostle of Jesus Christ, to those who have acquired a faith as precious as ours through the righteousness of our God and the Savior Jesus Christ: N.W.T.

(**Readers note:** It is important to add here that while this author does quote some from the N.W.T. he considers it to be unworthy of being called 'the Word of God' since the translation mostly is not true to the original text, especially texts which prove the Deity of our Lord Jesus Christ.)

Revelation 4:8-11

> And the four beasts...rest not day and night saying, Holy Holy Holy Lord God Almighty which was and is and is to come. And when those beasts give glory and honor and thanks to Him that sat on the throne who liveth forever and ever, the four and twenty elders fall down before him that sat on the throne and worship Him that liveth forever and ever and cast their crowns before the throne saying, Thou art worthy, O Lord to receive glory and honor and power for thou hast created all things, and for thy pleasure they are and were created.'

These verses point back to 3:14 which clearly identifies our Lord Jesus as the one in the beginning or dawn of creation who was the one who started creating all things, visible and invisible.

Revelation 3:14

> And unto the angel of the church of the Laodiceas write: These things saith the Amen, the faithful and true witness, the beginning of the creation of God.

Unfortunately I have heard some from the Watchtower society (not sure if this is their official position on this verse) claim this verse shows that 'God' created 'Jesus/Yeshua.' Nothing could be further from the truth! We have already shown in Revelation that Yeshua as coming in the clouds is clearly named as 'King of kings and Lord of lords, yea the Almighty (title to YHVH only and none else), and that He and He alone was the creator of all that there is, visible and invisible. To make such a preposterous claim is just as bad as saying this verse teaches Jesus 'created' God!

Next we need to go to one of the most powerful dialogs in the entire New Testament, one which flatly without question (of course except when questioned by those who have preconceived denial of the Deity of our Lord Jesus) gives our Savior's recognition of Him and the Father in heaven being one in the same personage. First though we must go to perhaps a parody example of that conversation say by a well known religious cult founder. Again, this example is **not** meant to claim this false cult founder claimed to be God (however he did claim to be God's prophet) yet just for the sake of argument, we shall pretend he did as follows. (Using John 14:3-11)

Charles Taze Russell and His Claim to Deity (A Parody)
"...so Russell said to His disciples, I will come again and receive you unto myself that where I am, there you may be also. *Doubting Thomas said to Charles Russell, Lord, we know not where you go and how can we know the way? Charles Russell said to Thomas I am the way the truth and the life, and no man cometh to the Father but by me. If you had known me you should have known my Father also, (I Charles Russell am the same as the Father, we are equals) and from here on Thomas you have known the Father YHWH and you do see Him now! Then Phillip said to the Lord Russell, show us the Father now and we will be satisfied. Lord Russell then said, Have I been so long time with you and yet have you not known me Phillip? He that has seen me has seen the Father we are equals and one in the same person! How can you say then 'Show us the Father?' Believe you not

that I am in the Father and the Father in me? (We are one in the same). The words that I speak to you I speak not of myself but the Father which dwells in me, He does the wonderful works I do. Believe me that I am in the Father and the Father is in me, or else believe the Father is in me for the very works which I do!

Now, for the sake of argument, *had the above parody actually been true*, this conversation between Russell and the disciples would irrefutably prove beyond any doubt that Russell was indeed God the Father come in the flesh. Any judge or jury when presented with this parody would agree that in it Russell claims to be the Father come in human form. This parody therefore clearly shows that the Lord Jesus Yeshua in John chapter 14 was clearly declaring His equality as YHVH! We are quite certain therefore that Mr. Russell now has a clear revelation of just who Jesus really was, being in the next world under the sentence of condemnation for rejecting the Deity of our Lord. Herein also our Lord reveals the unmistakable truth of the Trinity, which Watchtower (LDS and others) vehemently deny. Not three Gods, but one God which is manifested in three separate and distinct personalities, God the Father, God the Son, and God the Holy Spirit, one in three or three in one. Here in this chapter our LORD reveals the Father as being in heaven, where He is going, and then He proclaims that the Father is in Him, and yet the Spirit of God vs. 17, will come to indwell the disciples and all believers!

Following to be only fair to the Watchtower, we will give their version (which is not a direct accurate word for word translation of John 14:5-11). Unfortunately the New World Translation of the scriptures is not accurate, since much of it is paraphrased and not truly an accurate translation from the original languages. At least the A.V. 1611 gives italicized words in the English text to show when the translators added words to make the sentence readable. Bibles such as the Living Bible, Revised Version, Good News for Modern Man etc, are not actually translations, but rather paraphrased versions of ancient languages.

Charles Taze Russell and His Claim to Deity (A Second Parody)

Another excellent parody to show how clear the Word of God is concerning the deity of our Savior is found in Matthew 2:11 again using Russell in parody.

Matt. 2:8 &11

"And Herod called the wise men about the birth of Russell, he said, 'Go search diligently for the baby Charles Russell, and when ye have found Him bring Him bring me word again, that I may come and worship Him also… And when they were come into the house, they saw the young child with His mother and they fell down and worshipped Him and when they had opened their treasures they presented Him with gifts of gold and frankincense and myrrh.'

Now there is no doubt that the wise men that came to see our Lord Jesus/Yeshua would not have 'worshipped' the baby Jesus had He only been a created being equal to or on the same level as the Angels!

(It is well to remember Revelation 22:8-9 "And when I heard and saw, I fell down to worship at the feet of the angel who showed me these things. But he *said to me, "Do not do that. I am a fellow servant of yours and of your brethren the prophets and of those who heed the words of this book. Worship God." Our Lord Jesus throughout scripture commanded, deserved, and received worship, because He was literally God come in the form of a man!)

Watchtower New World Edition

Thomas said to him: "Lord, we do not know where you are going. How can we know the way?" Jesus said to him: "I am the way and the truth and the life. No one comes to the Father except through me.

If you men had known me, you would have known my Father also from this moment on you know him and have seen him." Philip said to him: "Lord, show us the Father, and it is enough for us." Jesus said to him: "Even after I have been with you men for such a long time, Philip, have you not come to know me? Whoever has seen me has seen the Father also. How is it you say, 'Show us the Father'? Do you not believe that I am in union with the Father and the Father is in union with me? The things I say to you I do not speak of my own originality but the Father who remains in union with me is doing his works. Believe me that I am in union with the Father and the Father is in union with me; otherwise, believe because of the works themselves.

1. The New World Translation is probably the most corrupt deceitful incorrect translation ever produced, truly a work of satanic origin since they represent our Lord Jesus as 'a god.' Correction…the New World Translation is not a 'translation' but rather an interpretation of what the Hebrew/Greek texts actually say. A true translation is a word for word meaning in one language being reproduced in another language with the same identical meaning. The Watchtower NWT is a total failure as a credible translation.

2. The New World so called translations at least are honest in making that point in the introduction to their Bible. I.e. They explain that the New World Testament is an 'interpretation' of what is said in the original language and not word for word translation. Amazing that the Watchtower 'Principles of Bible Translation' in the introduction to their supposed superior translation of the Bible, degrades the idea of a literal word for word translation from the original languages of God's Word into the English (etc.) language! They say (quoting)…"No modern language exactly mirrors the vocabulary and grammar of Biblical Hebrew, Aramaic, and Greek, so a word for

word translation of the Bible could be unclear or at times could even convey the wrong meaning. The meaning of a word or an expression may vary depending on the context in which it is used." So it is plain that they with their preconceived theology that our LORD Yeshua was only a created being, and not at all Deity that they can make the original language fit their theology! It is no wonder that their N.W.T skews the doctrine of the Trinity and makes our Savior just a created being.

The Watchtower Society has totally missed the crystal clear message of our wonderful Bible concerning the Deity of Jesus, especially one particular verse in Jeremiah chapter 23.

Jeremiah 23:5-6

Behold the days come saith the Lord, that I will raise to David a righteous Branch and a King shall reign and prosper and shall execute judgment and justice upon the earth. In His days Judah shall be saved and Israel shall dwell in safety: and this is His name by which He shall be called, 'JEHOVAH OUR RIGHTEOUSNESS.'

Needless to say this verse irrefutably refers to none other than our blessed Savior the Lord Jesus Yeshua Meshikha as one day He will rule over all the earth from His throne in Jerusalem! No one can possibly claim anything else. Going back to use our parody with Mr. Russell, suppose the Lord of Heaven said of him, "Mr. Russell you will be called 'JEHOVAH OUR RIGHTEOUSNESS.' If that were to happen then case closed, Mr. Russell would be YHVH in the flesh! Again to be fair to the Watchtower, following we quoted the same verses from their version and thankfully the truth is retained that Jesus is Jehovah YHVH.

Watchtower New World Translation

⁵ "Look! The days are coming," declares Jehovah, "When I will raise up to David a righteous sprout. And a king will reign and show insight and uphold justice and righteousness in the land. ⁶ In his days Judah will be saved, and Israel will reside in security. And this is the name by which he will be called: Jehovah Is Our Righteousness."

Yes…Yes…The Lord Jesus/Yeshua Is Jehovah COME IN THE FLESH literally Almighty God who came in the flesh!

Almighty God YHVH is a Triune God, one God manifested in the three persons of the Godhead, three in one or one in three!

The Doctrine of the Trinity is exonerated by scripture!

For more on the original New Testament go to www.aramaicnt.net for the works of Rev. Bauscher.